Recognition and Alleviation of

Pain *and* Distress

in Laboratory Animals

Committee on Pain and Distress in Laboratory Animals
Institute of Laboratory Animal Resources
Commission on Life Sciences
National Research Council

NATIONAL ACADEMY PRESS
Washington, D.C. 1992

NATIONAL ACADEMY PRESS • 2101 Constitution Avenue, NW • Washington, DC 20418

NOTICE: The project that is the subject of this report was approved by the Governing Board of the National Research Council, whose members are drawn from the councils of the National Academy of Sciences, National Academy of Engineering, and Institute of Medicine. The members of the committee responsible for the report were chosen for their special competencies and with regard for appropriate balance.

This report has been reviewed by a group other than the authors according to procedures approved by a Report Review Committee consisting of members of the National Academy of Sciences, National Academy of Engineering, and Institute of Medicine.

This project was supported by the National Center for Research Resources, National Institutes of Health (Grant R24 RR04523-02); American Veterinary Medical Association; Animal and Plant Health Inspection Service, U.S. Department of Agriculture (Grants 12-34-93-0090-IA and 12-34-61-001-GR); Center for Veterinary Medicine, Food and Drug Administration and Animal Welfare Information Service, National Agricultural Library, U.S. Department of Agriculture (Combined Grant 59-32U4-7-125); Association of American Veterinary Medical Colleges; Charles River Laboratories, Inc.; and E. I. du Pont de Nemours & Company. The views, opinions, and findings contained in this report are those of the committee and should not be construed as an official position, policy, or decision of the sponsoring organizations unless so designated by other documentation.

Library of Congress Cataloging-in-Publication Data

Recognition and alleviation of pain and distress in laboratory animals
/ Committee on Pain and Distress in Laboratory Animal, Institute of
Laboratory Animal Resources, Commission on Life Sciences, National
Research Council.
  p. cm.
Includes bibliographical references and index.
ISBN 0-309-04275-5
1. Laboratory animals—Diseases. 2. Pain in animals.
3. Laboratory animals—Effect of stress on. 4. Animal welfare.
I. Institute of Laboratory Animal Resources (U.S.). Committee on
Pain and Distress in Laboratory Animals.
  [DNLM: 1. Animals, Laboratory. 2. Animal Welfare. 3. Pain—
prevention & control 4. Stress—veterinary. QY 54 R311]
SF996.5R43   1992
636.088'5—dc20
DNLM/DLC
for Library of Congress   92-8266
                                                                    CIP

This book is printed with soy ink on acid-free recycled stock ♻ ◈

Printed in the United States of America

This report is respectfully dedicated to the memory of

HYRAM KITCHEN

September 24, 1932–February 8, 1990

Who dedicated his life to education for the benefit of animals

The National Academy of Sciences is a private, nonprofit, self-perpetuating society of distinguished scholars engaged in scientific and engineering research, dedicated to the furtherance of science and technology and to their use for the general welfare. Upon the authority of the charter granted to it by the Congress in 1863, the Academy has a mandate that requires it to advise the federal government on scientific and technical matters. Dr. Frank Press is president of the National Academy of Sciences.

The National Academy of Engineering was established in 1964, under the charter of the National Academy of Sciences, as a parallel organization of outstanding engineers. It is autonomous in its administration and in the selection of its members, sharing with the National Academy of Sciences the responsibility for advising the federal government. The National Academy of Engineering also sponsors engineering programs aimed at meeting national needs, encourages education and research, and recognizes the superior achievements of engineers. Dr. Robert M. White is president of the National Academy of Engineering.

The Institute of Medicine was established in 1970 by the National Academy of Sciences to secure the services of eminent members of appropriate professions in the examination of policy matters pertaining to the health of the public. The Institute acts under the responsibility given to the National Academy of Sciences by its congressional charter to be an adviser to the federal government and upon its own initiative to identify issues of medical care, research, and education. Dr. Kenneth I. Shine is president of the Institute of Medicine.

The National Research Council was established by the National Academy of Sciences in 1916 to associate the broad community of science and technology with the Academy's purposes of furthering knowledge and advising the federal government. Functioning in accordance with general policies determined by the Academy, the Council has become the principal operating agency of both the National Academy of Sciences and National Academy of Engineering in the conduct of their services to the government, the public, and the scientific and engineering communities. The Council is administered jointly by both Academies and the Institute of Medicine. Dr. Frank Press and Dr. Robert M. White are chairman and vice-chairman, respectively, of the National Research Council.

COMMITTEE ON PAIN AND DISTRESS IN LABORATORY ANIMALS

The Institute of Laboratory Animal Resources (ILAR) was founded in 1952 under the auspices of the National Research Council. Its mission is to provide expert counsel on the scientific, technologic, and ethical use of laboratory animals within the context of the interests and the mission of the National Academy of Sciences, which is to promote the application of science for the public welfare. ILAR promotes the high-quality and humane care of laboratory animals, the appropriate use of laboratory animals, and the exploration of alternatives in research, testing, and teaching. ILAR serves as an advisory group to the federal government, the biomedical research community, and the public.

COMMISSION ON LIFE SCIENCES

Preface

Animals contribute in important ways to the advancement of biology and to the understanding, prevention, and treatment of diseases of humans and other animals. Beginning with the work of Jenner, Pasteur, and Koch in animals over 200 years ago, vaccines have controlled or eliminated human scourges of smallpox, rabies, yellow fever, poliomyelitis, tetanus, and measles. Today, biotechnology and the use of transgenic animals offer new promise, not dreamed of just a few years ago, for the control of genetic disorders, cancers, and infectious diseases.

With the use of animals come responsibilities for their husbandry, care, and humane treatment. Elaborate safeguards have been implemented by the Animal Welfare Act and the Health Research Extension Act. Those acts give animal care and use committees power to oversee animal use and give investigators and veterinarians new responsibilities in ensuring that animals are not used for trivial purposes and that pain and distress are avoided or minimized. However, some animals used in research to prevent and reduce suffering of humans and animals will be subjected to conditions that cause them pain and distress. There is general agreement on the need to minimize pain and distress, but it has been difficult to bring the necessary melange of information together and to disseminate it throughout the scientific community.

For 40 years the Institute of Laboratory Animal Resources (ILAR) has developed guidelines for the humane use of animals in research, and in 1988 a group was assembled to advise ILAR on whether it should recommend strategies for complying with the new laws. Federal agencies, humane associations, academic institutions, private companies, and national biomedical associations that use or regulate the use of laboratory animals were consulted about the advisability of this project, and ILAR was encouraged to appoint an expert committee. The Committee on Pain and Distress in Laboratory Animals was thereupon formed and asked to prepare this guide as a method of communicating, to persons with widely differing backgrounds and interests, a deeply held ethical conviction that pain and distress in research animals must be avoided whenever possible and that, when it is not possible to avoid them, every effort must be made to recognize and alleviate them— both for the animals' well-being and to avoid effects of stress on the validity of research data.

The committee was asked to address both pharmacologic and nonpharmacologic methods of prevention and alleviation; to identify techniques or procedures likely to cause pain or distress; to develop a formulary of anesthetics, analgesics, and tranquilizers for laboratory animals; and to discuss known side effects of drugs or techniques that could confound research results. It quickly became clear to the committee that definitions would have to be developed for *pain*, *stress*, *distress*, *well-being*, and other terms. The committee proposes that stress progresses from acute stress to chronic stress and to distress when the physiologic cost of adapting becomes too high, at which time the animal manifests maladaptive behavior and intervention is indicated. *Professional judgment* (as used in the text to emphasize that the recommendations of this report should be interpreted in a manner most appropriate for the welfare of animals and the goals of science) is intended to refer to the collective wisdom and experience of the principal investigator, study director, attending veterinarian, and institutional animal care and use committee. Also, and perhaps most important, the committee felt that, to address nonpharmacologic means of prevention and alleviation, especially in regard to non-pain-induced (environmentally induced) stress, it would have to develop criteria and therapeutic strategies quite different from those used for the recognition and treatment of pain.

This volume is intended to increase the awareness and sensitivity of all those working with laboratory animals; provide a ready source of information on appropriate behavioral, biochemical, and physiologic indexes of pain and distress; and present and categorize the methods available for the prevention, reduction, or elimination of pain and distress in various laboratory animal species. The text is organized so as to summarize the scientific basis, recognition, alleviation, and control of pain, stress, and distress in laboratory animals. Chapter 7 discusses the use of euthanasia as a humane strategy of last resort for alleviating pain or distress and presents techniques to reduce stress in animals and in those who must euthanatize them.

General criteria for animal well-being are presented with the understanding that this involves more than good health and the absence of pain and distress and that the refinement of any procedure to improve the well-being of an animal is imperative. The refinement of experimental procedures, husbandry practices, and handling is consistent with the humane goals of Russell and Burch, who proposed the 3 Rs of replacement, reduction, and refinement to serve as responsible guide-lines for the use of animals. This volume focuses on the third R, refinement. We anticipate that this guide will be of interest to researchers, veterinarians, technicians, animal care and use committees, granting agencies, inspectors, site visitors, and others. The committee hopes that it will be useful in the planning or review of experimental procedures and housing and husbandry practices.

Shortcomings of the volume include incompleteness regarding drug side effects and how they can compromise the validity of research results. There is a paucity of information in this regard, but responsibility for it must be left to investigators. Perhaps future revisions of the volume can include more information on side effects and on the pharmacokinetic basis of dosage as additional relevant information becomes available. Readers should note that the report is intended to be a basic guide—it is not encyclopedic. Some readers will want more detailed discussions on some points or the inclusion of more drugs or animal species in the dosage tables. For those readers, an extensive bibliography is provided. The report does not treat the complex topics in cookbook fashion. Rather, it must be interpreted and applied with professional judgment.

The committee extends its appreciation to the contributors, sponsors, and reviewers of this volume; to Jennifer Fujimoto, Office of Campus Veterinary Services, School of Medicine, University of California, San Diego, for contribu-tions to the dosages and references for various species; and to Norman Grossblatt for editing the manuscript. Thomas L. Wolfle and the ILAR staff assisted the committee, and their dedication and contributions made this book possible.

Arthur L. Aronson, *Chairman*
Committee on Pain and Distress
in Laboratory Animals

Contents

xiii

Recognition and Alleviation of
Pain *and* Distress
in Laboratory Animals

1

Introduction

While pain and suffering in another being is, strictly speaking, unknowable, yet for practical purposes there are a number of lines of evidence of their presence and intensity which deserve attention. (Paton, 1984)

This book was prepared to help scientists, research administrators, institutional animal care and use committees, and animal care staff to address the difficult questions of the presence and alleviation of animal pain and distress. The authors believe that in most experimental and husbandry situations laboratory animals need not experience substantial pain or stress and that prevention and alleviation of pain and stress in laboratory animals is an ethical imperative. That view is shared by the public and Congress. The federal Animal Welfare Regulations (Code of Federal Regulations, Title 9), *Guide for the Care and Use of Laboratory Animals* (NRC, 1985), U.S. Public Health Service Policy for Humane Care and Use of Animals (PHS, 1986), and policies of the American Association for the Accreditation of Laboratory Animal Care *require* that veterinarians and investigators identify and eliminate sources of pain and distress, except those which are essential to the research in question and approved by the institutional animal care and use committee. Those regulations and policies also require that institutions develop programs for training personnel in procedures to ensure that animal pain and distress are minimized. The purposes of this book are to increase awareness of the sources and manifestations of stress and distress in laboratory animals and to increase ethical sensitivity in those who use and care for them. (It might also, indirectly, help to reduce the number of animals needed for experimental purposes: uncontrolled pain or distress can increase variability in experimental data and so require the use of more animals in a study for it to achieve statistical significance.) If this report improves investigators' awareness of their obligations for humane care and use of their research animals, it could even reduce the replication required to establish the generality of their scientific findings. This reduction, however, should always be consistent with the necessity to replicate and validate important scientific findings.

The book is developed around the sources and recognition of pain and distress and the pharmacologic and nonpharmacologic methods of avoiding and controlling them. It was not planned as a source of information on experimental design. Nor was it designed as a training document, although it is hoped that it will be useful for this purpose. (A recent report of the Institute of Laboratory Animal Resources might be of more direct assistance with the development of training and education programs [NRC, 1990].)

Chapters 2-4 focus on what is known about pain, stress, and distress in humans and animals. They constitute an introduction to Chapters 5-7, which provide specific recommendations for the care and use of laboratory animals.

GENERAL CONSIDERATIONS OF THE BIOLOGIC IMPORTANCE OF PAIN, STRESS, AND DISTRESS

The ability to avoid, escape from, or control pain and other inducers of stress and distress is critical to the survival and well-being of many animals (Phillips and Sechzer, 1989). Mechanisms that contribute to those abilities involve biochemical, physiologic, or psychologic changes and can be expressed behaviorally as homeostatic processes of adjusting to altered environmental conditions. Such behavioral processes can be short-term and adaptive or, as in cases of chronic pain and other potential sources of distress, can continue to the point where they become maladaptive. Maladaptive behaviors serve as important signs of distress in laboratory animals and indicate that intervention or scientific justification is required.

It is sometimes difficult to determine whether an animal is undergoing a normal process of adapting to a state of stress, for which intervention might not be indicated, or is in distress. Animal species differ in how they manifest distress, whether from pain or from other sources, and this complicates its recognition. But many signs of distress are shared by various animal species, and the tendency to highlight differences, rather than similarities, makes the task of recognizing it more complex than necessary. A comment on acute stress is in order. Under some circumstances, an animal can experience intense stress of short duration that (because it is brief) does not usually result in maladaptive behavior, although it might affect the animal's well-being adversely. Acute stress can also reduce the quality of research results. When stress is discussed in this text, the reader should consider whether the discussion applies to acute, as well as chronic, stress.

There is a lack of agreement on the meaning of such terms as *comfort, well-being, discomfort, stress, fear, anxiety, pain,* and *distress.* The terms and classification of syndromes presented here can be used provisionally and refined as additional information and understanding become available. The definitions that follow are presented as aids to the recognition of pain, environmental stressors, and the responses they produce. They should help to form the basis for the selection of appropriate pharmacologic and nonpharmacologic approaches to the prevention and alleviation of acute stress and distress. This document assumes that an animal's state can vary across a continuum from comfort through discomfort to distress, as evidenced by the appearance of physiologic changes and maladaptive behaviors. The state of an animal depends on the nature of the stressors, the degree of stress induced, and the animal's ability to respond in such a way as to maintain or return to a state of comfort.

DEFINITIONS*

Homeostasis refers to the tendency of the body to maintain behavioral and physiologic equilibrium.

Comfort is a state of physiologic, psychologic, and behavioral equilibrium in which an animal is accustomed to its environment and engages in normal activities, such as feeding, drinking, grooming, social interaction, sleeping-waking cycles, and reproduction. The behavior of such an animal remains relatively stable without noteworthy fluctuation.

Discomfort describes a minimal change in an animal's adaptive level or baseline state as a result of changes in its environment or biologic, physical, social, or psychologic alterations. Physiologic or behavioral changes that indicate a state of stress might be observed, but are not so marked as to indicate distress.

Well-being is the absence of too much stress. It describes a positive mental state that reflects the level of welfare and comfort of an animal (Tannenbaum, 1989, p. 247). It means more than the freedom from pain and distress. (See *comfort*, above.)

Stress[†] is the effect produced by external (i.e., physical or environmental) events or internal (i.e., physiologic or psychologic) factors, referred to as *stressors*, which induce an alteration in an animal's biologic equilibrium. (Some potential stressors are listed in Table 1-1 and described later in this chapter.) When a covert or overt response of an animal to a stressor is adaptive, the animal returns toward a state of comfort. Responses to stressors often involve changes in physiologic function (biochemical, endocrinologic, or autonomic), psychologic state, and behavior. An animal's response can vary according to its age, sex, experience, genetic profile, and present physiologic and psychologic state. Stress might not be harmful to an animal; it might evoke responses that neither improve nor threaten an animal's well-being. In some cases, environmental alterations that induce stress also initiate responses that have potential beneficial effects (Breazile, 1987). Some stress probably is necessary for well-being, if adaptation occurs with a reasonable

---

*We thank the American Veterinary Medical Association for permission to reproduce parts of this chapter with minor alterations from Kitchen et al. (1987).

†The committee has chosen not to use the term *suffering*, which is commonly used to refer to a broad spectrum of behaviors and emotions.

TABLE 1-1 Examples of Potential Stressors[a]

That Cause Physiologic Stress	That Cause Psychologic Stress	That Cause Environmental Stress
Injury ⎤	Fear	Restraint
Surgery ⎬ pain	Anxiety	Noise
Disease ⎦	Boredom	Odors
Starvation	Loneliness	Habitat
Dehydration	Separation	Ecology
		People
		Other species
		Chemicals
		Pheromones

[a]Note that pain is shown as resulting from physiologic stressors. It could also result from environmental stressors (e.g., chemical) and be potentiated by psychologic stressors (e.g., fear).

expenditure of energy. Whether stress and the responses or behaviors it induces should be considered adaptive should be based on professional evaluation and judgment.

Historically, the definition of stress has emphasized *physiologic characteristics*, especially those related to neuroendocrine systems (Cannon, 1929; Selye, 1974; Levine, 1985). However, it is now known that physiologic measures of stress might not be highly intercorrelated. Differences among physiologic measures in their relation to eliciting stimuli, time course, and adaptive implications have led most scientists to conclude that stress is not a discrete, *well-defined physiologic state* (Moberg, 1987). Stress remains a useful descriptor nonetheless: it provides a convenient means of identifying, describing, and summarizing important phenomena. For example, it is generally agreed that some environmental conditions or events can act as stressors, cause pronounced or persistent stress in an organism, and lead to alterations in neuroendocrine activities. The neuroendocrine changes can in some instances be severe enough to place the organism in a state of vulnerability to dysfunction or disease, although its behavior might not differ markedly from that typical of its species and might not yet have become maladaptive. Although there is no single measure or manifestation of such a state, some of the pathways and mechanisms through which it is brought about are reasonably well understood. Departures from a normal level of neuroendocrine activity can be considered as one kind of evidence of stress.

Distress is an aversive state in which an animal is unable to adapt completely to stressors and the resulting stress and shows maladaptive behaviors. It can be evident in the presence of various experimental or environmental phenomena, such

as abnormal feeding, absence or diminution of postprandial grooming, inappropriate social interaction with conspecifics or handlers (e.g., aggression, passivity, or
withdrawal), and inefficient reproduction; these phenomena are described in detail
in Chapter 4. Distress can also result in pathologic conditions that are not directly
evident in behavior, such as gastric and intestinal lesions, hypertension, and
immunosuppression. Maladaptive responses that briefly reduce an animal's
distress can be reinforced and thus become permanent parts of the animal's
repertoire and seriously threaten its well-being. Generally, any behavior that
relieves the intensity of distress is likely to become habitual, regardless of its long-
term effects on an animal's well-being. Examples of such behaviors are coproph-
agy, hair-pulling, self-biting, and repetitive stereotyped movements.

STRESSORS

Some potential stressors shown in Table 1-1 are described here.

• **Pain** results from potential or actual tissue damage. Pain can be considered
a potent source of stress, that is, a stressor. It can also be considered a state of stress
itself, however, and can lead to distress and maladaptive behaviors. Thus, whether
pain is viewed as a kind of stress or as a stressor depends on the point of reference.

The ability to experience pain is widespread in the animal kingdom and has
important survival value. For example, acute pain after injury or early in an illness
prompts an organism to take evasive action. Persistent or chronic pain *might* lead
to behaviors that spare an affected area or part. The responses to potential or actual
tissue damage are components of a complex experience that has sensory qualities
and affective or motivational and emotional consequences. *Injury* causes biologic,
chemical, or physical damage to tissue that is typically associated with pain and
therefore is a potential stressor. The effect of injury might be partially or completely
reversible; its extent can vary from little or no effect on normal function to marked
impairment.

Nociception is the peripheral and central nervous system processing of
information about the internal or external environment related to tissue damage,
e.g., quality, intensity, location, and duration of stimuli. Much of nociception takes
place at spinal and other subcortical levels, as evidenced by the existence of spinal
reflexes that do not produce awareness of pain. The encoding process can ultimately
result in pain, but is qualitatively different from the *perception* of pain
(nociperception), i.e., in the interpretation of sensory information as unpleasant.
Perception of pain depends on activation of a discrete set of receptors (nociceptors)
by noxious stimuli (e.g., thermal, chemical, or mechanical) and processing in the
spinal cord, the brainstem, the thalamus, and ultimately the cerebral cortex.
Nociceptive processing has access to areas of the brain that determine the degree of
unpleasantness of a pain experience, as well as its motivational and emotional
attributes. Thus, a simplified view of the pain experience includes two major
components: the sensory and the affective (Price and Dubner, 1977; Gracely et al.,

1978). This view is also reflected in the definition of pain (Mersky, 1979) adopted in 1986 by the International Association for the Study of Pain: "an unpleasant sensory or emotional experience associated with actual or potential tissue damage."

Acceptable levels of pain range from the threshold at which it is first detected to the upper limit of tolerance. The *pain threshold* is the point at which pain is first perceived during noxious stimulation. The pain threshold, of course, represents only minimal pain and is not commonly associated with stress or distress (Wolff, 1978). It has been shown to be essentially the same in humans and in warm-blooded vertebrate animals (Hardy et al., 1952; Vierck, 1976). (As discussed further in Chapters 4 and 5, the committee feels that the equivalence of the pain threshold across species is conceptually important for the recognition and alleviation of pain in diverse species. However, some feel that the equivalence is based on unproven assumptions about the measurement of stimuli and that similarity among species cannot be known with certainty.)

Pain tolerance is essentially the upper limit or highest intensity of pain that will be accepted voluntarily. Pain tolerance varies in a given organism under different circumstances and within and between species, depending on a number of factors, such as the experimental situation, motivation, previous painful experience, and the level of anxiety or fear. The *pain sensitivity range* is the difference between the pain threshold and pain tolerance (Wolff, 1978).

Although animals lack the ability to communicate their pain verbally, they can exhibit behaviors and physiologic responses similar to those of humans in response to noxious or tissue-damaging stimuli. The behaviors include simple withdrawal reflexes, vocalization, and learned responses ranging from guarding an injured limb to attempting to escape, avoid, or terminate a painful stimulus. The physiologic responses include those associated with an acute stress reaction, such as changes in blood pressure and heart rate and the activation of the pituitary-adrenal axis (see Chapter 4).

Succeeding chapters will review the stress and potential distress that can be induced by pain and the choice of pharmacologic and nonpharmacologic methods to alleviate pain and pain-induced distress.

• **Anxiety** and **Fear** are emotional states that are traditionally associated with stress. They can be adaptive, in that they inhibit an organism's actions that could lead to harm or cause it to act in ways that allow it to escape from potentially harmful situations; they can also potentiate the affective quality of pain.

Anxiety and fear are not sharply differentiated behaviorally or physiologically. The causes of anxiety are usually assumed to be less specific than the causes of fear. For example, an animal in a new environment or experiencing a novel but benign procedure might be described as anxious. *Fear* is more often used to describe an emotional state that results from an experienced or known danger in the immediate environment. For instance, a dog that has gone through a painful experience in a particular setting might vocalize or try to escape when placed in that setting again. Thus, *fear* usually refers to a focused response to a known object or previous experience, whereas *anxiety* usually refers to a generalized, unfocused response to the unknown.

• Of all stressors to which laboratory animals are likely to be exposed, those caused by environmental influences—**Environmental Stressors**—are probably the most pervasive. They include cage or habitat design, feeding routines, handling techniques, noise, odors, investigative procedures and techniques, interactions with humans, interspecies interactions, and conspecific social interactions, including dominance-subordination relationships. Those and other undetermined stressors can interfere with animals' well-being, in ways that are sometimes manifested as an inability to express species-typical behaviors. Many other environmental stressors are elaborated in Chapter 3. The identification and control of these stressors from the animals' or species' perspective constitute good husbandry and are a primary responsibility of all who care for or use animals in a laboratory setting.

DISTRESS MODELS

Table 1-1 lists representative examples of three categories of stressors—psychologic, physiologic, and environmental. Any stressor can initiate stress in an animal and, depending on previous states and experiences, have the potential to affect homeostasis profoundly. The categories of stressors are not mutually independent, and stressors can overlap and interact within and between categories.[*] Interaction of several stressors can act to increase or decrease the net effect of stressors and the resulting stress. Chapters 2 and 3 describe stressors and their potential action as sources of stress and distress for laboratory animals.

DISTRESS NOT INDUCED BY PAIN

An animal's state can vary across a continuum from comfort to distress (Figure 1-1). When an animal is in a state of comfort or discomfort, homeostatic (adaptive) processes tend either to maintain the state of comfort or to return the animal toward a state of comfort. Stressors do not pose a threat to the animal as long as it can maintain an adaptive equilibrium. When that is no longer possible, the animal enters a state of distress, in which its behavior and physiology become maladaptive. No single behavioral or even physiologic measure is an unequivocal indication of distress. Distress should be inferred when there is converging evidence, rather than from a single sign. It is here that judgment and knowledge of an animal and its species-typical behaviors play an important role in determining the state of the animal.

---

[*]Interaction is especially likely between pain and physiologic stressors and between psychologic and environmental stressors.

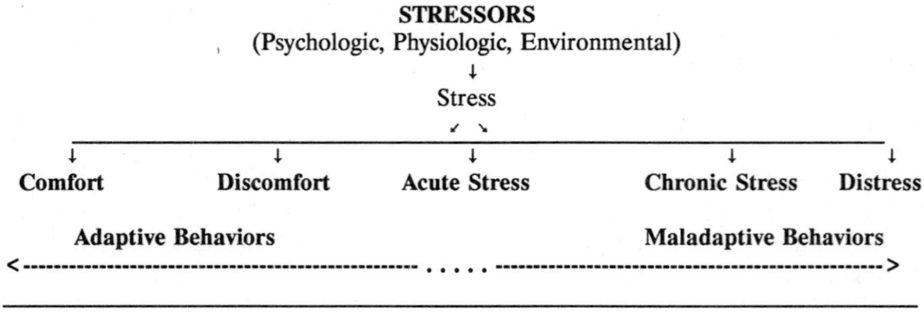

STRESSORS
(Psychologic, Physiologic, Environmental)
↓
Stress
↙ ↘

↓	↓	↓	↓	↓
Comfort	**Discomfort**	**Acute Stress**	**Chronic Stress**	**Distress**

Adaptive Behaviors   **Maladaptive Behaviors**

<--- · · · · · -->

FIGURE 1-1   Model of distress not induced by pain. Stressors, leading to stress, can initiate various states in an animal from comfort to distress. Adaptive stress will not interfere with an animal's state of comfort or well-being. When an animal is experiencing distress, maladaptive behaviors result, varying in range and severity with increasing distress.

DISTRESS INDUCED BY PAIN

More is known about the role of pain as a stressor than about the roles of other stressors. A model of distress induced by pain is shown in Figure 1-2. The figure shows how pain initiates stress, which leads either to adaptation and comfort or to maladaptive behaviors and distress. It depicts the sensory and affective components of pain and suggests a dominant role of affect in leading to distress.

The distress models described here provide a framework for discussing the sources of stress and distress and the patterns of adaptive and maladaptive behaviors that can result (Chapter 3). An understanding of those patterns will be important for the prevention of pain and distress, for the recognition and assessment of pain and distress (Chapter 4), and for the control of pain (Chapters 5) and the control of distress (Chapter 6) in experimentation, testing, and educational projects involving animals. Chapter 7 reviews specific euthanasia techniques to be used at the termination of an experiment or when animals are in distress that cannot be alleviated; it also reviews the psychologic effects on personnel who carry out euthanasia and presents some recommendations to minimize the emotional impact on personnel involved.

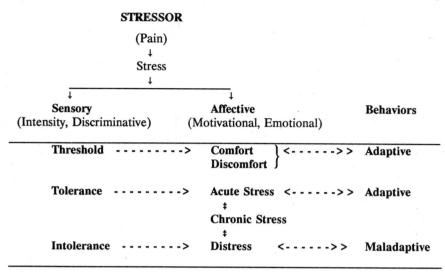

FIGURE 1-2 Model of distress induced by pain. Note relationship between sensory discriminative component and affective emotional component. Sensory component of pain ranges from threshold to tolerance and then intolerance. In affective components, intensity of pain can proceed from a state of comfort to distress. Arrow paths indicate flow from sensation to affect to behaviors. This is the normal case, but under some conditions, behaviors can influence affect and thus modify the sensation. Double arrows emphasize that behavior is primarily influenced by affect. (Direction of flow indicates schematized concept only, not neural pathways.)

2

The Basis of Pain

This chapter reviews the basis of pain in animals from a comparative perspective and uses the definitions of *pain* and *nociception* provided in Chapter 1. Scientific understanding of pain in animals has been derived in part from comparative studies and from studies in animals in which pain was the experimental variable. Much of what we know about the central nervous system (CNS) mechanisms of pain is derived from animal studies, and they will continue to be important in increasing our understanding of pain mechanisms in both humans and animals (Kitchell et al., 1983). This chapter therefore makes comparisons between humans and animals and refers to experimental pain paradigms in animals as a model for discussing avoidance, recognition, and alleviation of pain.

PERIPHERAL MECHANISMS OF NOCICEPTION

An understanding of how the pain sensing system works is critical for controlling pain. There is a long-standing controversy about how signals related to tissue damage are transmitted to the CNS (Dubner et al., 1978). Earlier theories proposed that pain resulted from the excessive stimulation of all types of peripheral receptors and that the brain merely received information about the threat of tissue damage (for review, see Melzack and Wall, 1965). An alternative theory proposed that specialized receptors in peripheral tissues encoded features of tissue-damaging stimuli—their quality, location, intensity, and duration. The theory of neuronal specialization in the pain sensing system has received considerable support from the finding of specialized receptors that signal tissue damage (Dubner and Bennett,

1983; Willis, 1985) or intense stimulation of muscle or visceral tissue. Those peripheral receptors are called *nociceptors*, and they can be classified according to how they respond to intense mechanical, thermal, or chemical stimuli. With minor exceptions, nociceptive fibers have finely myelinated or unmyelinated axons. Most, if not all, mammalian species have such nociceptors. The most extensively studied nociceptors are the ones that have myelinated axons and respond only to intense mechanical or mechanical and thermal stimuli and the so-called polymodal nociceptors, which have unmyelinated axons and respond to mechanical, thermal, and chemical stimuli. The myelinated nociceptors appear to encode signals related to pricking first-pain sensations produced by noxious mechanical or thermal stimuli. Second-pain sensations, which follow first-pain sensations and have a burning quality, appear to be encoded by signals arising from unmyelinated nociceptors (Price et al., 1977).

Tissue injury produces a state of hyperalgesia (excessive sensitivity to pain) at the site of injury with increased sensitivity to stimuli and sometimes spontaneous pain sensations. Those alterations have distinct parallels to a phenomenon called *sensitization* observed in nociceptors. After repeated exposure to noxious heat stimuli, nociceptors exhibit lower thresholds, increased sensitivity to stimuli that exceed their thresholds, and spontaneous activity. Both mechanical-thermal nociceptors and polymodal nociceptors mediate, in part, the hyperalgesia produced by mild thermal injury in humans (Meyer et al., 1985).

MEDIATORS OF INFLAMMATION AND PAIN

Sensitization and hyperalgesia involve the release of various chemical mediators (Hargreaves and Dubner, 1991). A simplification of this process is as follows: Cell injury results in the release of prostaglandins, leukotrienes, bradykinin, substance P, and other autacoids. These products, acting in concert with one another, contribute to inflammation and associated sensitivity and pain, as evidenced by increased vascular permeability, increased leukocyte migration, and increased sensitivity of nociceptors.

Products of arachidonic acid metabolism are mediators of inflammation. Arachidonic acid is released after cell injury from phospholipids embedded in cell membranes. Metabolism proceeds in two directions: The enzyme cyclo-oxygenase converts arachidonic acid to prostaglandins, which increase vascular permeability, activate leukocyte migration, and sensitize nociceptors; and the enzyme lipoxygenase results in the formation of leukotrienes, some of which increase vascular permeability and chemotaxis of polymorphonuclear leukocytes. Leukotriene B4 results in the release from leukocytes of chemicals that produce sensitization of nociceptors.

Another important inflammatory mediator is bradykinin. The precursors of bradykinin circulate in the blood and are released into the tissue whenever there is damage. Injury results in an increase in tissue acidity and in the conversion of the enzyme prekallikrein to kallikrein. Kallikrein then acts on the bradykinin precursor kininogen to release bradykinin into the tissue. Bradykinin increases vascular permeability, promotes vasodilatation, induces leukocyte chemotaxis, and activates nociceptors. The action of bradykinin on nociceptors is potentiated by prostaglandins present in injured tissue.

A third important inflammatory mediator, substance P, released from the peripheral endings of nociceptors after injury, results in plasma extravasation and induces the release of histamine from mast cells and of serotonin from platelets.

The various mediators of inflammation not only increase the excitability of nociceptors in the tissue space, but also result in the release from nerve endings of neuropeptides, such as substance P and calcitonin gene-related peptide, that participate in the development of the inflammatory process. The clinical significance is that blockage of the development of the mediators can reduce pain; the most notable example is the effectiveness of nonsteroidal anti-inflammatory drugs (e.g., aspirin) in inhibiting the conversion of arachidonic acid to prostaglandins and thereby producing analgesia. (See Chapter 4 for additional information on biochemical mediators of pain and stress.)

DORSAL HORN NOCICEPTIVE MECHANISMS

Two general classes of neurons in the spinal and medullary dorsal horns receive input from peripheral nociceptors (reviewed by Dubner and Bennett, 1983). One class, *nociceptive-specific neurons*, respond only to intense forms of mechanical, thermal, and other noxious stimuli and receive input exclusively from nociceptors. The second class, *wide-dynamic-range neurons*, are activated by hair movement and weak mechanical stimuli, but respond maximally to intense stimulation, such as a pinch or pinprick. Many wide-dynamic-range neurons respond to noxious heat; they receive input from low-threshold mechanoreceptors, as well as from nociceptors. Recent studies have shown that wide-dynamic-range neurons, but not nociceptive-specific neurons, participate in the encoding process by which monkeys perceive the intensity of noxious stimuli (Dubner et al., 1989).

Some wide-dynamic-range and nociceptive-specific neurons are components of long projection pathways that relay information to the thalamus and from there to the cerebral cortex. Others are local-circuit neurons whose axons are confined to the dorsal horn. Four major long projection pathways appear to be important in nociceptive transmission (Figure 2-1): the spinothalamic tract, the spinocervical tract, the spinomesencephalic tract, and the dorsal column postsynaptic spinomedullary system (Dubner and Bennett, 1983). The relative importance of each system is not entirely clear and likely depends on the species. The evidence of a role in pain transmission is most extensive for the spinothalamic tract, which for a long time was considered the only long projection system encoding information about actual or potential tissue damage. In humans, the importance of the spinothalamic tract is demonstrated by the profound, short-term analgesia that occurs caudal to its transection. That the analgesia is often not complete suggests

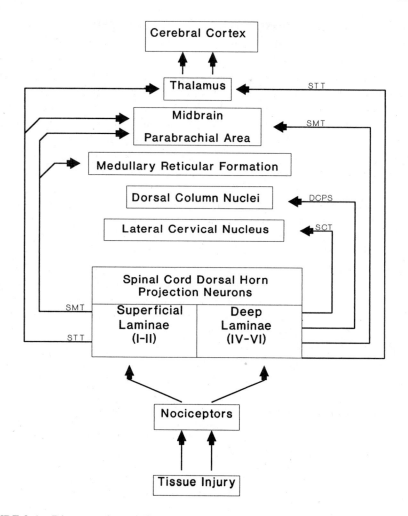

FIGURE 2-1 Diagram of ascending nociceptive pathways originating in spinal cord and medullary dorsal horns. Four major long projection pathways are spinothalamic tract (STT), spinocervical tract (SCT), spinomesencephalic tract (SMT), and dorsal column postsynaptic spinomedullary system (DCPS). Origins and terminations are shown.

that other systems are also involved in nociceptive transmission. The spinocervical tract is variable from species to species, larger in cats and much smaller in monkeys and humans. Spinocervical tract neurons are mainly low-threshold mechanoreceptive neurons, responding best to light touch or hair stimulation; a few are nociceptive neurons almost entirely of the wide-dynamic-range type. The spinomesencephalic tract is known to be present in rats, cats, and monkeys and sends bilateral projections to the parabrachial region of the midbrain that includes the parabrachial nuclei, nucleus cuneiformis, and the lateral part of the ventral periaqueductal gray (Hylden et al., 1989). The dorsal column postsynaptic spinomedullary system has axons ascending mainly in the ipsilateral dorsal funiculus and terminates in the dorsal column nuclei in the medulla. In the lumbar enlargement of cats and monkeys, dorsal column postsynaptic spinomedullary system neurons are as numerous as cat lumbar spinocervical tract neurons. Most dorsal column postsynaptic spinomedullary system neurons are in the same lamina IV band as spinocervical tract neurons. The dorsal column postsynaptic spinomedullary system is composed mainly of wide-dynamic-range and low-threshold mechanoreceptive neurons with a few nociceptive-specific neurons.

Neurotransmitters that participate in the processing of nociceptive information have been studied extensively in the dorsal horn (Dubner, 1985; Ruda et al., 1986). Enkephalin and dynorphin, two opioid peptides that are the products of different genes, are found in the dorsal horn. Opioid-containing neurons can function as inhibitory or excitatory chemical mediators in local-circuit and long projection neurons. During inflammation, there is an increase in synthesis and content of both dynorphin and enkephalin in the dorsal horn (Iadarola et al., 1988; Draisci and Iadarola, 1989), and these changes involve both long projection neurons and local-circuit neurons (Nahin et al., 1989). The opioid neural circuitry in the dorsal horn is related to one mechanism of analgesic action of morphine, the most widely used opioid drug. It appears that opioid drugs alter the perceived intensity of noxious stimuli at the level of the dorsal horn by suppressing the activity of nociceptive wide-dynamic-range neurons (Oliveras et al., 1986). The ability of morphine and other opioids to act directly on the dorsal horn has led to their epidural and intrathecal administration in clinical situations (Yaksh and Rudy, 1978).

THALAMOCORTICAL MECHANISMS

The presence of terminations of the spinothalamic track in the ventrobasal and medial thalamus leaves little doubt that the thalamus plays an important role in pain (Willis, 1985). There is considerable evidence that neurons in the ventrobasal thalamus respond to tissue-damaging stimuli and have characteristics similar to those of the wide-dynamic-range and nociceptive-specific neurons in the spinal dorsal horn. It is now accepted that most neurons in the posterior nucleus of the thalamus respond to tactile inputs, but the role of this nucleus in nociception is not clear. The medial thalamus also receives input from the spinothalamic tract, and cells in this region have been reported to respond to noxious stimuli. The more medial nuclei project to wide areas of the cerebral cortex and to parts of the limbic system involved in motivation and affect; therefore, they probably play a role in the motivational-affective aspects of pain, rather than in its sensory-discriminative aspects. However, nociceptive neurons in the ventral posterior thalamic nuclei project to the primary somatosensory cortex, and that suggests their participation in the processing of the sensory features of noxious stimuli. More recently, it has been shown in trained monkeys that wide-dynamic-range neurons in the cerebral cortex participate in the encoding process by which monkeys perceive the intensity of noxious heat stimuli (Kenshalo et al., 1988). Earlier findings in humans that lesions of the postcentral gyrus reduce pain and that stimulation of the exposed somatosensory cerebral cortex can sometimes produce pain constitute additional evidence of a role of the cerebral cortex in the elaboration of pain sensations.

DESCENDING CONTROL MECHANISMS

The above findings support the involvement of specialized neural pathways in the encoding of pain sensations. However, those pathways are not immutable and are subject to considerable modulation by descending control systems from many other brain sites (reviewed by Dubner and Bennett, 1983).

Electric stimulation in the midbrain periaqueductal gray and the midline raphe nuclei in the medulla (Figure 2-2) inhibits the activity of dorsal horn wide-dynamic-range and nociceptive-specific neurons (Mayer et al., 1971; reviewed by Mayer and Price, 1976; Wolfle and Liebeskind, 1983). Stimulation in those sites inhibits a wide variety of behaviors and reflexes induced by noxious stimuli. The direct administration of opioids at the sites with microinjection also suppresses dorsal horn activity and behaviors and reflexes produced by noxious stimuli. The

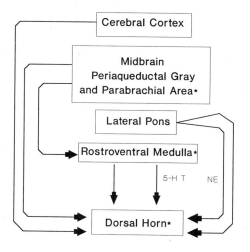

FIGURE 2-2   Diagram of some major descending pathways that modulate nociceptive output from dorsal horn. Neurochemical specificity of some pathways is known. NE, norepinephrine; 5-HT, serotonin (5-hydroxytryptamine). Some sites (*opioid-containing local neurons present) contain opioid-rich local-circuit neurons involved in modulatory effects.

administration of naloxone, a specific opioid antagonist, can block the effects of both electric stimulation and opioid administration. In humans, electric stimulation in periaqueductal and periventricular structures produces an analgesia that can be attenuated by the administration of naloxone (e.g., Hosobuchi et al., 1977).

On the basis of such findings, it was proposed and later established that the CNS has its own naturally occurring opioids. It is now known that there are three major families of endogenous opioid peptides, each the product of a different gene: the enkephalins, the dynorphins, and the endorphins. In addition to the opioid peptides, which probably contribute to analgesic processes in the CNS in a more localized fashion via relatively short neural circuits, longer, chemically specific descending neural systems containing norepinephrine or serotonin play major roles in the modulation of pain (Figure 2-2). Descending norepinephrine- or serotonin-containing pathways, originating in the medulla and pons, affect the output of wide-dynamic-range and nociceptive-specific neurons and alter responsiveness to noxious inputs.

The multiple descending circuits, probably interacting with opioid peptide-containing neurons in the spinal cord or brainstem, underlie the behavioral modulation of pain. In a more general sense, the descending and local circuits are mechanisms by which an organism extracts useful information from its environment. The identification of the multiple pain-suppressing pathways has led to a search for their physiologic role under natural conditions. Some forms of stress, fear, exercise, and disease states (e.g., hypertension), including pain itself, appear to activate the pathways. However, we still have only a few clues as to the role of the descending control systems in the processing of sensory information under ordinary behavioral conditions.

3

The Basis of Stress and Distress Not Induced by Pain

INTRODUCTION

The nonpain causes of stress in laboratory animals can be grouped into three general categories: experimental methods, external (environmental) sources, and internal, physiologic (endocrinologic, biochemical, or neurologic) causes. Those categories can be used to facilitate consideration of the issue, but are not mutually exclusive. For example, a stressful experiment might later trigger a fear response in an animal the next time it is removed from its cage, even in the absence of external stressors; focusing on the method of removal from the cage will probably not relieve the fear. Similarly, stress produced by social isolation, social aggression, inappropriate caging, or careless husbandry practices might be manifest when an animal is used in an experiment; addressing the experimental design is not likely to be very useful. And experimental and environmental stresses are likely to cause changes in physiologic functions.

Environmentally caused stress, unlike pain, can have vastly different causes. No common pathway exists by which all non-pain-inducing stressors exert their influence. Rather, it appears that environmental stress results from a combination of various stressors and their impact on an organism's ability to adapt to them. Recognition, or anticipation, that a particular event will be perceived as an important stressor by an animal requires knowledge not only of the stressor, but of the species-typical responses to situations and of the experience of the particular animal.

It should be obvious that stress can result from husbandry practices, experi-

17

mental procedures, social interactions, feeding regimens, lighting, odors, noises, and so forth. It is not possible to list all possible stressors, because the variety of experiences and responses of animals is vast. This chapter will therefore concentrate on environmental and ecologic factors that have been demonstrated in humans and animals to be important contributors to stress. They are not all-inclusive causes of stress, but are intended to represent major categories that can be useful options for consideration. The categories are derived from what is known about causes of stress in animals in general, including wild animals and humans, as well as laboratory animals. Even ecologic stressors that have no obvious impact on laboratory animals (e.g., predator-prey relations and foraging) have implications for research animals that should be considered.

Stress is a normal feature of life and serves important adaptive functions. The physiologic processes involved in the flight of an antelope being chased by a cheetah and in the cheetah that pursues it are examples of the normal adaptive functions of stress. Those processes allow both animals to maximize their physiologic resources in a situation of vital concern to each of them. Stress is also common in captive environments. It can be produced by pain and by extreme variations in ambient temperature, illness, demanding tasks, and almost any situation that an animal perceives as threatening or that puts it in a state of uncertainty and conflict (Hennessy and Levine, 1979; Weinberg and Levine, 1980). It is important to recognize the presence and varied sources of stress for ethical reasons and because the physiologic changes associated with stress are likely to affect experimental data. Research designs and experimental procedures should be planned to minimize stress.

Although stress has normal adaptive functions, stress in captive environments can lead to pathologic changes, such as gastric ulcers, and to outcomes that are maladaptive. When that occurs, it can be said that the animal is not only stressed, but distressed. As stated in Chapter 1, distress is a state in which an animal is unable to adapt completely to stressors; it differs from stress only in the manifestation of maladaptive behaviors or other pathologic processes.

Pain is an example of a stressor. The primary biologic function of pain is to signal potential or actual tissue damage. An animal in pain characteristically shows postures or behaviors that alleviate or terminate the pain (see Chapter 4). When an animal in pain is prevented from assuming those postures or performing those behaviors, or if they are not effective, it might show maladaptive responses. It is then in distress.

Most environmental stressors lack the specificity of pain, both with respect to the sensory systems that mediate them and with respect to the physiologic and behavioral reactions they elicit. The potency of many stressful conditions or events can change quickly. Moreover, one animal adapts readily to a particular environmental stressor, and another does not. The difference can be the result of habituation, a learned association with other environmental events, or the acquisition by one animal, but not the other, of the ability to cope with the stressful circumstance.

This discussion underscores the basic principle that all environmental effects are revealed by *individual* animals—an obvious point that is often disregarded. To be valid, judgments made about such matters as the suitability of caging arrangements, feeding regimens, and the behavioral or psychologic needs of captive animals must be based on familiarity with the normal behavior of individual animals and a professional evaluation of the situation approached from individual animals' points of view.

ECOLOGY AND THE CAPTIVE ENVIRONMENT

As a first step in approaching the environment from the animal's point of view, the distinction made by field biologists between habitat and ecology is useful (Vernberg and Vernberg, 1970). *Habitat* refers to all measurable aspects of the physical and biotic environment. Habitats are what we usually have in mind when we think of environments. They are described without reference to any particular class of organisms on which they might impinge. A monkey, an ocelot, and a sloth occupying the same tropical forest share the same habitat. Ecology, however, always presumes a specific animal (or other biologic entity). It is the focus on the interrelationships between the entity and its environment that characterizes the ecologic perspective. To the extent that the monkey, the ocelot, and the sloth are active at different times during the daily cycle, differ in their social lives, and differ in the foods and other vital resources they require and in how they take these resources from the environment, they differ in their ecologies.

The distinction between habitat and ecology can also be applied to captive environments. Although the habitat of the captive environment is dictated largely by human design, it is useful to consider it in terms of the kind of ecology that it provides. Attention is thereby focused on the nature of the relationships that a specific animal establishes with its surroundings.

It is essential to bear in mind that ecologic relationships are inherently reciprocal or transactional. The animal and the captive environment are each organized, dynamic entities and should be looked at in terms of their own needs and objectives. The captive environment is designed and maintained by humans for their own purposes. It not only imposes constraints on the kinds of relationships with the habitat that are possible for the animals residing therein, but also reflects the interests of the human proprietors. Those interests are usually mixed and might not be wholly compatible. For example, they might include some combination of economic concerns, the purposes for which the human organization exists (e.g., research, animal production, or public exhibition), and the desire to maintain animals in conditions that are conducive to good health, that minimize distress, and that foster their overall well-being.

To the extent that humane concerns and animal well-being are at issue, those responsible for the care and management of animals should consider the captive environment from the standpoint of the resident animals; that is, it is the animals' ecology, not their habitat, that provides the relevant perspective. From that perspective, the significance of physical structures and routine procedures, as well as infrequent environmental events, will be different from the significance based on the habitat perspective.

How does one approach the captive environment from the ecologic perspective of the animals? Professional judgment, empathy, and intuition are indispensable aids; but they are also very fallible guides and cannot always substitute for more reliable and objective kinds of information.

At the most basic level, birds and mammals—indeed, all animals—have fairly strict requirements with respect to nutrients, water, ambient temperature, humidity, illumination, background noise, and light-dark cycles. Although specific recommendations for dealing with those aspects of an animal's ecology in a captive setting are more often based on professional judgment and opinion than on systematic research, their importance for well-being is widely recognized, and they are usually treated straightforwardly as requirements of good husbandry (see NRC, 1985).

Other ecologic characteristics of captive environments are considered less often, although they can have an important influence on stress and distress (Hughes and Duncan, 1988). On the basis of general ecologic considerations, it can be assumed that the following constitute six major dimensions that are relevant to stress and distress for species housed in a captive environment: relations with conspecifics, predator-prey relations, shelter, spatial architecture, feeding and foraging, and environmental events. Each is discussed in some detail below.

RELATIONSHIPS WITH CONSPECIFICS

Other members of the same species as a given animal usually have significant influences on stress and distress in the animal. The nature of those influences varies widely among species and among individuals within species. Age, sex, and early experience have powerful effects on the extent to which animals will seek, tolerate, or be distressed by the close presence of other members of their species. In many species, seasonal and other cyclic variations in the reproductive state of an animal can affect its social tolerance and sociability.

In determining the potential contribution of social factors to stress and distress, one must consider social space and crowding, deprivation, and social stimulation.

Social Space

The tendency of animals to space themselves in relation to each other is a general feature of social behavior (Waser and Wiley, 1979). The most common means of establishing and maintaining social spacing are overt aggression (e.g., biting and scratching) and aggressive displays (e.g., threat postures and vocalizations). Spacing behavior can be organized with respect to a specific location or with respect to the area surrounding an animal, regardless of where it happens to be. Dens, nest sites, and the location of a food source are examples of particular places where intruders are likely to meet with an aggressive response. The space that an animal maintains between itself and other animals can be called its personal space. Intrusion of other animals into this area is not tolerated and leads to aggression toward the intruder or withdrawal by the animal intruded on. The size of personal space varies with species and sex and with the familiarity of the intruder. More gregarious species have smaller personal space; that is, they are more tolerant of intruders than species that are normally solitary. Tolerance for the proximity of other animals is usually greater between members of opposite sex than between members of the same sex, between immature animals than between animals that are reproductively mature, and between immature and reproductively mature animals than between animals that are reproductively mature. Tolerance is likely to be least between unfamiliar, reproductively mature animals of the same sex, particularly males. The expression of species differences in personal space are not limited to relations with conspecifics; they can also be reflected in the way animals react to proximity of people and to petting and other forms of human contact (Hediger, 1955).

Crowding

Crowding represents more than an encroachment on personal space. Experimental studies with various species of rodents have shown that, when the number of animals confined to a particular area increases beyond a critical point, normal patterns of social organization and social interaction break down, aggression increases, and reproductive failures that are traceable to physiologic causes occur. Information on other vertebrate species, although less complete, is in general agreement with those findings (Archer, 1970).

Deprivation

Social deprivation includes several kinds of conditions or procedures. Although they share the element of restricting or preventing social access to other animals, their consequences and their bearing on questions of stress and distress in captive animals are not the same. The most important factors are related to the age at which deprivation occurs and the nature of the animal's previous social experience.

Nurturance and early social experience: The young of many animal species depend on their mothers for warmth and protection. Newborn mammals universally depend on their mothers for food and often receive from their mothers various forms of stimulation that influence their behavioral and physiologic development. For example, olfactory stimulation from a mother rat contributes to the integration of nursing in infants and modulates their activity levels (Hofer, 1978). The basic requirements for food and warmth are universally recognized and are routinely met in the laboratory when contact with the mother is not possible.

Beyond those basic needs, the young of many mammalian species require stimulation from conspecifics, or from appropriate social substitutes, to ensure normal behavioral development and adult social competence (Newton and Levine, 1968). Although there is no question that the behavior of animals deprived of such stimulation from birth is atypical, it has not been established that they are chronically stressed. However, the behavior of many adult animals deprived of social interaction in early life is obviously maladaptive. Self-mutilation, hair-pulling, stereotypic behaviors, extreme timidity or aggressiveness, and inability to mate or provide adequate care to offspring are examples of maladaptive behaviors that might result from social deprivation and be taken as de facto evidence of distress. A concern with the well-being of captive animals and with their long-range utility for research and reproduction warrants provision of opportunities for social interaction of developing animals with members of their own species and in some cases with humans (e.g., in the case of dogs), unless deprivation of such opportunities is a carefully articulated requirement for a specific research project.

Disruption of infant-parent bonds: Given the opportunity, the young of some avian and mammalian species will form an emotional bond or attachment to their mother or an appropriate substitute. In those species, social deprivation occurs if an immature animal that has formed such a bond is separated from its attachment figure (Reite and Field, 1985). The acute responses indicate stress. Whimpering and other high-pitched vocalizations typically increase and are accompanied by corresponding changes in general activity, heart rate, and cortisol concentrations. Those reactions are adaptive under natural circumstances, in that they attract caregivers and prepare a young animal for vigorous action. If prolonged, however, they can become distressful and lead to increased vulnerability to disease. Distress is likely to be less intense and persistent in animals that no longer depend entirely on an attachment figure for nutritional and emotional support, that have access to familiar companions or a substitute attachment figure, and that remain in familiar surroundings after separation.

In some species, such as primates, mothers also show an emotional response to separation from their infants. Their behavioral and physiologic reactions appear to be similar to those of an infant, although less persistent and intense.

Disruption of adult bonds: The term *social deprivation* can also be applied to adult animals that are separated from familiar companions. The question of whether social bonds or emotional attachments that develop between adults are similar in form or intensity to attachments between parent and young has seldom been examined systematically. On the basis of comparisons between two primate species, one monogamous and the other polygamous, it appears that pair-living monogamous adults respond to separation in a manner that is similar to, but less intense and prolonged than, the response of immature animals to separation from an attachment figure. In contrast, polygamous adults show no reaction to separation from familiar companions of the opposite sex (Mendoza and Mason, 1986).

Positive Social Stimulation

Play, grooming, huddling, and merely sitting quietly in physical contact are normal and recurrent activities for many highly social animals. Such activities are sought, and they have been shown in some species to have reward properties—e.g., dogs (Stanley and Elliot, 1962), primates (Mason, 1967), and rats (Latané and Hothersall, 1972). They have also been shown to have immediate effects on emotional arousal. For example, being groomed, petted, or stroked can bring about a prompt reduction in signs of distress in various species (Mason, 1965; Gantt et al., 1966). Stroking and handling by humans can be a practical and effective technique for calming animals in situations where they are distressed, particularly animals that have been positively socialized by humans. The procedure should be used with caution, however, with animals that are not accustomed to human contact or animals that might transmit disease.

It is reasonable to assume that being able to engage in positive social behaviors will contribute to an animal's comfort and well-being, although there are few pertinent systematic data. It is also common to assume that depriving an animal of the opportunity to engage in such behaviors is an important source of stress. Although that assumption seems plausible, it has not been adequately tested and cannot be accepted uncritically as applying to all animals. The importance or attractiveness to an animal of opportunities for positive social stimulation will depend on its species, age, and prior social experience. Whatever distress results from depriving an animal of positive social stimulation will presumably be least severe for species or individual animals that are weakly gregarious, fearful, or highly aggressive, for older animals, and for animals whose social experience has been narrow.

PREDATOR-PREY AND DEFENSIVE RELATIONSHIPS

Predation concerns the capture and consumption for food of one animal by another. Predator-prey relationships are a normal aspect of the natural history of virtually all species. Some biologic groups near the top of the food chain are primarily predators (e.g., many carnivores); others are primarily preyed on (e.g., rabbits and most ungulates); and many species are both predators and prey (e.g., rats, pigs, and primates). Because of the close association of predation with evolutionary success, avoidance of and defense against predators and capture of prey have had profound influences on the evolution of animal behavior (Bertram, 1978).

Although actual predation is ordinarily not a factor in well-managed captive environments, evolved patterns of predator-prey behavior can enter into an animal's relations with caretakers, with other species of animals that it encounters, and with members of its own species. Under normal conditions, the intrusions are unlikely to pose a serious threat to the well-being of captive animals. Nevertheless, sensitivity to the conditions that elicit predatory tendencies or defensive reactions in captive animals might help to prevent or manage stress or distress.

A particularly potent elicitor of predatory behavior is movement. It is conceivable that frequent intermittent provocation and frustration of predatory tendencies can be a stressor for some highly predatory species. But it is more likely that predatory behavior will be an indirect cause of stress, because it is unknowingly triggered by humans and punished because it is misinterpreted. For example, specific actions by caretakers or handlers might accidentally elicit a predatory attack in an otherwise trustworthy animal; because the response is unanticipated, painful to the handler, and seemingly unprovoked, it could cause the person to retaliate, or at least put a strain on future relations with the animal. The threshold for predatory behavior is likely to be lower in an animal that has been deprived of food or is anticipating being fed.

Defensive reactions, like predatory behavior, are usually immediate reactions to specific "releasing" stimuli. An animal might signal that it is in a defensive mood by changes in posture (e.g., crouching), facial expression (e.g., exposing teeth), vocalizations (e.g., growling), and behavioral signs of autonomic arousal (e.g., piloerection, defecation, urination, and trembling). Any event that an animal perceives as threatening can provoke defensive behavior. Such events are not uncommon in captive environments. Defensive reactions can be elicited by the mere presence of a perceived predator; but if exposure is repeated or prolonged and there are no additional adverse consequences, the response is likely to dissipate through habituation. Any abrupt, careless, or unusual action by caretakers or handlers can provoke a defensive reaction, even if the action causes no pain. The animal's response might consist of vigorous efforts to escape, immobility ("freezing," or feigning death), or attack, depending on the species and circumstances. Many animals will bite if pressed in situations where they cannot escape. Defensive reactions are more likely to occur when an animal is anxious or fearful, as in a novel setting, or is being physically restrained, undergoing an unfamiliar procedure, or in pain. The presence of newborn animals can also lower the threshold for defensive reactions—particularly in females, but also in males of some species.

SHELTER

The availability of nest boxes, nesting materials, dens, and the like is widely recognized as essential for some species to carry out various biologic functions (e.g., birth and early infant care in rats, mice, rabbits, and some nonhuman primate species). If such facilities are provided permanently, they will be used regularly and routinely by some species. The presence or absence of dens and cover can affect stress and distress in ways that cannot be anticipated. For example, domestic rats that have had access to burrows reportedly are more difficult to handle and more aggressive toward conspecifics than those raised in open cages (Price, 1985). The findings suggest that dens or cover can help an animal to cope with stress by giving it a place to hide, but make it less able to cope in other circumstances. These comments are intended to suggest possible sources of stress for some animals, not as a blanket recommendation for shelters, dens, or covers for all laboratory animals that might use them in their natural habitat.

SPATIAL ARCHITECTURE

Space is an important dimension in the daily lives of animals. The volume of space used, the distribution of activities within a defined area, and the kinds of activities that occur vary with species (Waser and Wiley, 1979). For arboreal animals, perches, swings, and climbing devices can increase the effective volume of space and help to promote gross motor activity and possibly contribute thereby to the health of the animals. Running wheels and appropriate areas for defecation and urination, digging, dust-bathing, claw-sharpening, gnawing, and the like can also provide outlets for species-typical activities.

It is generally assumed that caging arrangements that deprive an animal of the opportunity to engage in species-typical activities are stressful and lead to the development of pacing and similar stereotyped motor patterns, to self-mutilation, and to other undesirable behaviors (Morris, 1964; Meyer-Holzapfel, 1968). That is possible, but it is difficult to establish specific cause-effect relations. The features of the cage that are supposedly the problem are seldom known with certainty, and it is rarely possible to relate particular patterns of abnormal behavior to specific deficiencies in cage design. Furthermore, although some behaviors might constitute distorted or compensatory responses to the frustration of a particular species-typical "need," as is generally supposed, others might simply be common elements in the species' normal repertoire that are readily available and easily performed in the captive environment. Even if a given pattern of behavior is abnormal for a species, it is often not clear whether it should be regarded as a sign that the animal is in a state of distress or has developed an adaptive mode of coping with constraints or tensions caused by the captive environment (Price, 1985; Dantzer, 1986).

At our current state of knowledge, the goal should be to provide environments that enable and promote species-typical activity. However, decisions to provide environmental devices to encourage and sustain species-typical activities should be made carefully. The benefits of a particular addition might be negligible or have only short-term effects. Possible benefits should also be weighed against the costs of constructing, installing, and maintaining the equipment and against the problems that the devices might create in decreased sanitation and increased risk of injury to the animals.

FEEDING AND FORAGING

Research on captive animals has emphasized nutritional requirements while neglecting other aspects of feeding behavior. Captive animals are typically offered a well-balanced diet on an established schedule; the procedure is efficient and economical, and it places no demands on the individual animal.

The situation is quite different in natural environments. It is obvious that carnivores and omnivores are different from frugivores and herbivores, not only in what they eat, but in virtually every aspect of their feeding behavior. *Feeding ecology* refers to all attributes of an animal's relation with the environment from the standpoint of gaining sustenance. The amount of time spent in searching for food, food preferences and aversions, the ways foods are gathered and prepared, the frequency and size of meals, and degree of tolerance of monotonous diets are all facets of feeding ecology (Schoener, 1971). Sensitivity to a species' feeding ecology can provide useful clues as to how an animal will respond to the diet and feeding routines of a captive environment (Breland and Breland, 1961). Failure to recognize the importance of ecologic factors in the feeding situation and to take them into account can lead indirectly to conditions that contribute to stress and threaten well-being.

The amount of experimental data on feeding behavior in captive environments is much greater for the domestic variety of the Norway rat than for other species. The rat is a classic omnivore and is timid in its approaches to novel foods, so extrapolation from it to other species should be viewed with caution. In the absence of firm evidence on most species, the following generalizations are offered as tentative guidelines.

Adaptability

Most species show considerable flexibility in accommodating to the foods and feeding routines of a captive environment. Assuming that an animal is regularly provided a fresh, palatable diet that is adequate in quality and quantity to meet its nutritional needs, established feeding regimens are seldom a direct cause of stress or distress.

Response to Novel Foods

Some species are very cautious about new foods; a sudden change in the taste, appearance, odor, or texture of foods might reduce intake to stressful levels, even though the nutritional value of the new food is as good as or superior to that of the former. If new foods are introduced, they should be introduced gradually. The new food and the standard diet should both be offered until there is evidence that adequate amounts of the new food are being eaten.

Need for Variety

The monotony of an unchanging diet can reduce food intake and lead to weight loss and stress. Variety in the diet can be a stimulant. Broad changes in the composition of the daily ration might not be advisable, however, from the standpoint of either animal nutrition or economy. Treats and tidbits offered as occasional supplements can serve as "appetizers" and lead to increased intake of the standard food.

Free Choice

Allowing animals to choose freely from a broad range of foodstuffs differing in nutritional value can result in nutritional imbalances. Moreover, rodents fed ad libitum have shorter lives, have a greater incidence of neoplasia, and might develop more disease (Abelson, 1992). Animals are likely to select foods on the basis of superficial qualities, such as odor and taste, rather than on the basis of nutritional properties.

Food Wastage

Nonhuman primates are wasteful feeders. An animal might take several pieces of food and discard all but one or drop a piece of food after one or two bites and then select an identical new item and treat it in the same manner. As a result of such behavior, a food container can be emptied quickly. If discarded food falls through the cage floor and cannot be retrieved, the animal might not consume enough to sustain itself, even though an adequate quantity of food is provided initially. It cannot be assumed that an animal will eventually learn to stop dropping food.

Transition from Milk to Solid Foods

Weaning and the transition from milk to solid foods can be stressful. The transition to solid foods is a developmental process that takes time to complete. Weaning by the biologic mother can be stressful for both parties. It is accomplished gradually, however, and usually is not finished before the young animal is able to sustain itself entirely on solid foods. That observation has important implications for animals that are being hand-reared or whose access to solid foods is restricted for research purposes. The rate of the transition to solid foods is influenced by a number of factors and varies widely with species. Guinea pigs are capable of sustaining themselves on solid foods at birth; rabbits, rats, cats, and dogs take considerably longer; and in some primate species weaning is not completed before the sixth month of life or later. The observation that an immature animal is ingesting small quantities of solid foods is not a reliable indication that it is capable of maintaining itself without milk. The rate at which a young animal makes the transition from milk to solid foods depends on such factors as the quantity and quality of solid food provided, the time available to acquire an appetite for solid foods, and facilitation provided by observing the feeding behavior of older animals.

Food Searching

Searching or foraging for food is a normal part of the feeding behavior of many species. The activity of searching for food appears to be somewhat independent of the immediate need for food, its consumption, or its availability. Whether depriving a species of the opportunity to search for food causes stress or distress has seldom been examined experimentally. It seems unlikely that it constitutes an important source of stress or distress for most species. Nevertheless, there is some evidence that providing materials that encourage foraging can have indirect benefits, such as reducing aggression, boredom, or other undesirable behaviors in animals living alone or in social groups (Chamove et al., 1982; Bloomstrand, 1987; Line and Houghton, 1987; Chamove and Anderson, 1988; Lindberg and Smith, 1988; Moazed and Wolff, 1988; Novak and Suomi, 1988; Bloom and Cook, 1989; Bloomsmith, 1989; Boccia, 1989; Maki et al., 1989; DiGregorio, 1990; Visalberghi and Vitale, 1990; Bayne et al., 1991).

Predictability of Feeding Times

Animals on a fixed feeding schedule come to anticipate the time of day when food will be provided. Substantial deviations from established schedules can cause frustration accompanied by increased activity in stress-responsive physiologic systems. The frustration appears to be a reaction to the deviation from the regular feeding time, rather than a response to food deprivation itself.

ENVIRONMENTAL EVENTS

For the most part, captive animals are in a passive position with respect to environmental events. Management procedures and routines might be designed to minimize stress and distress of animals, but the animals themselves are not in control of these activities and usually have little, if any, influence on how they are carried out. That contrasts sharply with the natural situation, where animals have responsibility for their own maintenance and well-being. In a natural setting, animals must become familiar with their surroundings, investigate objects or events that are out of the ordinary, and take the initiative in dealing with their problems.

For most animals, the elements of novelty and predictability of environmental events and the ability to control the environment are related to stress and distress in captive settings. Experiments on the effects of novelty, predictability, and lack of control have been oriented mainly toward understanding the causes and consequences of stress. Many studies have used electric shock as a stressor and have examined the effects of predictable vs. unpredictable electric shock and of providing animals with the means of escaping or avoiding shock or having control over it. The effects of novelty have been investigated by placing animals in wholly unfamiliar settings or presenting new stimuli in familiar settings. In general, novelty, the absence of predictability, and the lack or loss of control cause an increase in the activity of stress-responsive physiologic systems (Hennessy and Levine, 1979; Weinberg and Levine, 1980). Similarly, the human handling of most animals reduces anxiety and fear, but the handling of animals unaccustomed to it can be a profound stressor (Gärtner et al., 1980). In that regard, it is wise to follow practices established by the institution or the research protocol in order to minimize stress in the animals and reduce variability between them.

Many of the conditions that have been shown to be stressful in experimental research have parallels in common colony management procedures. Changing cages, confinement in a strange setting, physical restraint, venipuncture, injections, and modifications of established maintenance routines are examples of events that confront animals with novelty, unpredictability, and loss of control and that are potentially stressful. The magnitude and duration of the stressful effects of those events are influenced by many factors, including the number of previous exposures an animal has had to the particular conditions, its early experience, its temperament, and the skill and sensitivity of the persons carrying out the procedures.

Predictability and a sense of control over research environments can be provided by enabling animals to adapt to novel environments. Adaptation is particularly important before animals are placed on experimental protocols that require restraint, for example. Letting dogs adapt to people through a process of socialization at appropriate ages and frequencies serves a similar purpose and reduces the fear and anxiety that might occur when they are approached or restrained by people.

Transportation has long been known to cause stress in animals. Whether the stress is due to alterations in circadian rhythms, changes in familiar surroundings, noise and vibration, extreme temperature, dehydration, or some other cause is not known. However, standard practices should be implemented to ensure that transportation to and with a research institution follows accepted procedures and that newly arrived animals are given enough time to recover and to adapt to the new environment before they are placed in an experiment (Landi et al., 1982). Scheduling of direct flights, provision of enough food and water and of ventilation, and avoidance of extremes in temperatures to which the animals have not adapted are essential.

Boredom is the response to the opposite of excessive novelty and unpredictability. It is caused by too little variety and change. The immediate surroundings of many captive animals seem barren, unchanging, and nonstimulating. Few things provoke their attention or maintain their interest, and they can do little to relieve the apparent monotony of the situation.

It has been known for many years that animals are actively curious about their surroundings (Berlyne, 1960). Depending on the species, they will explore novel settings; manipulate puzzles, levers, chains, and ropes; look at photographs; and in various other ways voluntarily expose themselves to fresh and unusual objects and stimuli. They will also take advantage of the opportunity to control environmental events by such actions as turning lights and sounds off and on and performing actions that cause food to be delivered, even when adequate amounts of the same food are freely available.

That animals engage in those activities does not necessarily mean that they have a strong need to do so. Many domesticated and wild animals spend long periods during the waking day lying down, sleeping, or sitting quietly. Nevertheless, by analogy with modern society's view of human nature, it might seem that a stimulating and responsive environment is a common requirement for well-being. Whether that is generally the case for captive animals has not been established, and opinions vary (Wemelsfelder, 1990).

The assumption of a true need for varied activities and stimulation is the basis for current efforts at environmental enrichment. Enrichment can take various forms. One of the most common approaches is to provide toys, puzzles, or mechanical devices that animals can use if they choose, without forcing them to do so. Food is also used as a reward or incentive to encourage the use of enrichment devices (Markowitz, 1978, 1982; Line, 1987; Beaver, 1989; Fajzi et al., 1989; Bayne et al., 1991).

The systematic study of environmental enrichment is just beginning, and many questions need to be investigated. Although it seems plausible that boredom is a serious problem for some captive animals and can cause stress or distress, there is little objective supporting evidence. Most likely, reactions to monotony will vary with species or strain of animal, with age, and with previous experience, but these possibilities have not been thoroughly investigated. The design and assessment of enrichment devices are also in their early stages. Designs are based mainly on intuition and guesswork, and there is no way to know in advance that a particular device will be used as expected or whether, if it is used, it will make a positive contribution to well-being. As with other cage amenities, the benefits of enrichment devices need to be established and weighed against the attendant costs and risks.

RESEARCH APPROACHES

Several generalizations about the effects of captive environments on stress and distress can be made. It is well established that the species or strain of an animal (its genetic makeup) is critical. Temperament and responsiveness differ widely, even among closely related species. Species that have departed only slightly from the wild state are likely to react more strongly to stressful conditions and to find more conditions stressful than species that have been selectively bred for adaptiveness to captive environments (Price, 1984). A wealth of scientific information indicates that an animal's early experience can have profound and lasting effects on the kinds of situations it responds to as stressful and on the nature of its response (Newton and Levine, 1968). Age, sex, and seasonal variations are other factors known to affect the intensity of stress and distress and the situations that elicit these reactions.

Most research thus far has been oriented toward theoretical issues, and this work needs to continue. But future research must explicitly include concern with identifying the actual conditions in the captive environment that are sources of stress and distress and the steps that can be taken to prevent or alleviate the conditions. That concern should be clearly reflected in research designs.

The aim of experiments on stress and distress in captive environments is not to create a facsimile of the natural habitat in appearance or function, but to identify aspects of captive environments that impinge most directly on processes related to stress and distress and to determine how they do so. For example, one might expect a species that was solitary, timid, and heavily preyed on in its natural environment to react more intensely to the close presence of conspecifics, to handling and other routine caretaking procedures, and to being placed in novel settings than a species that was highly social, bold, and predatory. That is a testable possibility.

It is equally important that the effectiveness of various living arrangements and techniques in alleviating stress and distress be investigated experimentally (see Chapters 4 and 5). Realistic recommendations based on experimental findings will need to consider economic and other practical concerns, in addition to matters related strictly to animal well-being. Although objective assessments of the sources and alleviation of stress and distress in captive animals constitute an ambitious and expensive program, it is clearly feasible and well within the capabilities of contemporary scientific methods.

Ideally, the scientific investigation of stress and distress would be based on explicit and universally agreed-on definitions of these conditions. But such a connection has proved elusive. It is hoped that the definitions and concepts of stress and distress formulated in this report will take the terms one step closer to being readily useful in describing clinical signs.

Physiologic assessments of stress have been carried out for a number of years, and a considerable amount of information is available on (often weak) interrelations between various measures and their functional significance. However, we need much more information on the interrelations between behavioral, physiologic, biochemical, reproductive, and clinical signs of stress. The association between behavioral and physiologic measures is not always strong, and in some cases these measures might not even be associated (e.g., Weinberg and Levine, 1980).

The importance of firm baseline data (norms) is recognized; the conditions that contribute to departures from baseline values and the implications of such departures for physical health, reproduction, and vitality have been explored for some species in reasonable detail and are the objects of current research. That does not imply that stress research is in a mature state, particularly as it is related to matters of well-being, but knowledge and theoretical issues regarding stress are more completely developed than those regarding distress.

4

Recognition and Assessment of Pain, Stress, and Distress

This chapter builds on the definitions provided in Chapter 1 and the discussions of pain and environmental sources of stress and distress in Chapters 2 and 3. It is intended to enable readers to recognize and assess pain, stress, and distress in laboratory animals for the purposes of developing therapeutic, environmental, and behavioral strategies for decreasing them and lessening their impact on experimental data. The recognition of pain, pain-induced distress, and non-pain-induced distress in animals is ethically necessary for proper clinical management of animals to ensure their well-being and to reduce research variability.

RECOGNITION AND ASSESSMENT OF PAIN

The responses of humans to potential or actual tissue damage are parts of a complex experience that has sensory qualities and motivational and emotional consequences. The nervous system encodes the sensory features of tissue-damaging stimuli, such as their quality, intensity, location, and duration. What we perceive results in behavioral and physiologic responses that are under the influence of emotional, motivational, and cognitive processes. Noxious or tissue-damaging stimuli are unpleasant and can evoke strong negative feelings that include memories of previous discomfort, cultural beliefs about pain, and our awareness that pain can imply serious harm to our body. Thus, as described in Chapters 1 and 2, a simplified view of the pain experience includes two major components: sensory and affective or emotional.

There should seldom be a question about the possibility that a laboratory animal is in pain, if basic principles are followed. *U.S. Government Principles for Utilization and Care of Vertebrate Animals Used in Testing, Research, and Training* (IRAC, 1985) states that "unless the contrary is established, investigators should consider that procedures that cause pain or distress in human beings may cause pain or distress in other animals." Experimentally induced pain is ordinarily predictable and either avoidable or relievable, according to the requirements of the research protocol. But unforeseen circumstances might place an animal in unexpected pain, and there must be ways to recognize it.

In evaluating procedures that cause pain and distress, one should justify the procedures and their potential benefits to humans or animals. Societal concerns about the welfare of animals used for experimental purposes necessitate that standards be developed to take into account all relevant information, including scientific data and observations from both biologic and behavioral sources. Guidelines should be established that ensure relief from pain or distress in any study (Dubner, 1987; Montgomery, 1987). Pain, stress, and distress that are not produced specifically for study should be viewed as unnecessary, unwanted, data-compromising side effects (Amyx, 1987; Spinelli and Markowitz, 1987). It must be emphasized that stress can still affect experimental results even if an animal under stress seems to be adapting and is manifesting no maladaptive behavioral or physiologic signs.

CLINICAL APPROACHES TO THE ASSESSMENT OF PAIN

One of the more important responsibilities in the use of animals for biomedical research is to recognize clinical signs associated with pain. Without a knowledge of their normal and abnormal behavior and appearance, assessment of pain in animals is difficult, because animals are unable to communicate in ways in which they can be readily understood by people (Hughes and Lang, 1983; Soma, 1987).

An important step in determining that an animal is in pain is the recognition of a departure from the animal's normal behavior and appearance (Morton and Griffiths, 1985; Dubner, 1987; Kitchen et al., 1987; Dresser, 1988). Well-being is usually associated with species-typical behavior and is used as a descriptor for healthy animals that are adapted to their environment (however, see Chapter 3). A well animal will play with its cagemate or handler, exhibit normal curiosity through explorations, keep itself well groomed, appear to be in good health, grow normally, and have normal reproduction.

There are no generally accepted objective criteria for assessing the degree of pain that an animal is experiencing (Morton and Griffiths, 1985), and species vary widely in their response to pain. However, some behavioral signs are usually associated with pain (Table 4-1). Animals often communicate pain by their posture.

TABLE 4-1   Signs of Acute Pain[a]

Sign	Explanation
Guarding	Attempting to protect, move away, or bite
Vocalization	Crying out when palpated or forced to use affected area
Mutilation	Licking, biting, scratching, shaking, or rubbing
Restlessness	Pacing, lying down and getting up, or shifting weight
Sweating	In species that sweat (horses)
Recumbency	Unusual length of time
Depression	Reluctance to move or difficulty in rising
Abnormal appearance	Head down, tucked abdomen, hunched, facial distortion, or pallor

[a]Reprinted with permission from Soma, 1987.

For example, an animal with abdominal pain might sit hunched up or hold a limb in an abnormal position. Occasionally, an animal in severe pain flails about, struggles, writhes, or has extensor rigidity. The affected area could be wet from repeated licking, and licking can progress to self-mutilation and chewing at the affected area. Wounds—self-inflicted, from other animals, or from surgery—can appear red and swollen. Assessment of signs of less severe pain involves at least some subjective interpretation and requires careful clinical observation and familiarity with animals' responses to similar situations (Soma, 1987). Animals in pain often display an appearance that is best described as an "absence of normal behavior." Normal behavior can be characterized by various species-typical actions, such as cats' response to stroking, goats' head pushing, and pigs' or primates' general activity and vocalization. When an animal is in pain, these aspects of behavior can be strikingly absent; the animal might withdraw to the rear or corner of its cage or become aggressive and show signs of attack, or it might even become listless, inactive, or immobile (Flecknell, 1985).

Assessing Vocalizations

Vocalizations are natural reactions to pain in many animals and can be used as a guide to the degree of pain (Lefebvre and Carli, 1985; Cooper and Vierck, 1986). An animal might squeal, bark, or otherwise phonate when handled. Vocalization also includes groaning, grunting, whimpering, whining, and growling. Some noises indicative of pain are characteristic of a particular species; they are usually more than momentary and are often repeated. Vocalizations associated with pain can be used to measure an animal's reactivity to pain. Attempts to restrain pigs and nonhuman primates that are in pain can cause vocalizations, but these and other animals also vocalize in association with feeding or the presence of a familiar person or strangers. In many species, vocalizations differ enough to convey specific meanings to careful observers. However, vocalizations are not definitive and reliable indicators of pain in some animals, and the absence of vocalization is not an invariable indicator of the absence of pain. Furthermore, many vocalizations of rodents, and possibly other animals, are at frequencies above the hearing range of people.

Responses to Handling

In any clinical examination of an animal, inspection and palpation are important. Before restraint is applied, an animal's posture or movement should be observed for evidence and localization of pain. Once the animal is restrained, a complete physical examination should be conducted (see Pare and Glavin, 1986, for a review of the stress caused by restraint). Knowledge of the animal's normal response to handling is desirable, because individual animals can respond differently. An animal in acute pain might have increased muscle tone, show reluctance to be handled, and guard the painful area. It might turn its head toward the source of pain when the area is touched, attempt to bite its handler, or cry out if the painful site is manipulated. Those signs can often be associated with activation of the sympathetic nervous system as manifested in increased heart and respiratory rate, dilated pupils, increased body temperature, sweating, and muscle tremors.

Elicitation of a response associated with pain, such as movement of the head toward the area being palpated, might be necessary to show that the animal is in pain and to locate the painful area. Palpation of the abdomen often causes the muscles to tighten, and the animal might grunt, squeal, or attempt to bite.

Acute Pain

Acute pain plays a protective role: it warns about injury. Acute pain can be produced by transient stimuli, such as venipuncture or brief electric shock. Such pain produces a stress response, but usually does not lead to distress, because the pain is short-lived. In the face of such phasic tissue-damaging stimuli, animals are generally able to adapt their behavior and accept their discomfort. Acute pain also can result from an inflammatory process that originated in damaged tissue, surgery, traumatic injury, or exposure to metabolic, bacterial, or viral disease or toxins. Behavioral responses vary among breeds and species, but the classic signs of inflammation are universal: pain, edema, redness, increased temperature, and loss of function. Those signs are mediated by the release of chemical mediators, such as bradykinin, prostaglandins, leukotrienes, substance P, serotonin, and histamine (Chapter 2). The inflammatory process produces increased neural activity originating in the response of receptors to tissue-damaging stimuli.

Chronic Pain

Chronic or persistent pain is different from acute pain and can be harder to recognize, because its onset is slow, its intensity is likely not constant, it is not necessarily associated with an obvious pathologic condition, and it usually does not serve any vital protective function. It is also more likely to lead to distress and maladaptive behavior.

Animals in chronic pain can be divided into three broad categories: those with a known pathologic condition (e.g., arthritis, cancer, or injury), those in which an organic cause of the pain can be inferred from the results of the clinical examination and history (e.g., pain of musculoskeletal origin, peripheral nerve damage, or disease of the central nervous system), and those with signs that resemble signs in one of the other categories but without obvious cause. Animals in all three categories can exhibit signs of psychologic or psychosocial dysfunction.

Some signs are likely to be common to chronic pain of any origin. They include decreased appetite, weight loss, reduced activity, sleep loss, irritability, and decreased mating and reproductive performance (Soma, 1987). Alterations in urinary and bowel activities and lack of grooming are signs often associated with chronic pain, and tearing and lacrimal accumulations around the eyes should be noted. Animals whose pain is chronic or that are moribund might exhibit reduced body temperature, a weak, shallow pulse, and depressed respiration—signs of a poor prognosis.

Chronic pain of the musculoskeletal system is fairly easy to recognize because of lameness or reluctance to move. Some chronic conditions can cause an animal to harm itself; e.g., licking can progress to rubbing, chewing, or scratching, and occasionally self-injury becomes so severe as to mask the cause. Even if a cause is identified and corrected, maladaptive behaviors might persist and require careful diagnosis and treatment (Chapter 5).

Classification of Procedures Likely to Cause Pain

As with all surgical procedures, appropriate anesthesia should be used to render the animal insensitive to pain. However, the postsurgical period is most likely to be associated with pain; pain should be expected, and appropriate use of analgesics should be planned and described in the research protocol. Table 4-2 lists signs, degrees, and durations of pain associated with various classes of surgical procedures.

The Committee on Animal Research of the New York Academy of Sciences (NYAS, 1988) has developed guidelines for research that uses animals. Table 4-3 lists examples of experiments of various types and some ethical considerations relevant to them. The guidelines are of value to scientists who are designing experiments and to institutional animal care and use committee (IACUC) members who are trying to identify painful and distressful procedures.

TABLE 4-2 Signs, Degree, and Length of Surgically Produced Pain[a]

Surgical Site	Signs of Pain	Degree of Pain	Length of Pain
Head, eye, ear, mouth	Attempts to rub or scratch, self-mutilation, shaking, reluctance to eat, drink, or swallow, reluctance to move	Moderate to high	Intermittent to continual
Rectal area	Rubbing, licking, biting, abnormal bowel movement or excretory behavior	Moderate to high	Intermittent to continual
Bones	Reluctance to move, lameness, abnormal posture, guarding, licking, self-mutilation	Moderate to high: upper part of axial skeleton (humerus, femur) especially painful	Intermittent
Abdomen	Abnormal posture (hunched), anorexia, guarding	Not obvious to moderate	Short
Thorax	Reluctance to move, respiratory changes (rapid, shallow), depression	Sternal approach, high; lateral approach, slight to moderate	Continual
Spine, cervical	Abnormal posture of head and neck, reluctance to move, abnormal gait— "walking on eggs"	Moderate to severe	Continual
Spine, thoracic or lumbar	Few signs, often moving immediately	Slight	Short

[a]Based on observations of dogs.

SPECIES-TYPICAL SIGNS

Species-typical signs should be taken into account in an assessment of pain. Experience suggests strongly that some signs are often associated with pain. No sign, however, can by itself be regarded as diagnostic of pain, because similar signs occur in conditions in which pain is unlikely. Signs are not all present at one time, and those present on one examination can change by the next. Signs of pain should therefore be considered as a complex group and evaluated together.

TABLE 4-3 Guide to Types of Experiments That Are Considered Painful or Stressful[a]

Types of Experiments	Examples of Procedures	Special Ethical Considerations
A. Experiments on *unanesthetized* animals not expected to have pain and/or distress.	Naturalistic observations of behavior (e.g., in the field, in nonextreme environments); social interactions and noninvasive procedures; EEG, EKG, EMG in trained animals; minimal nutritional modifications; conditioning or training procedures using appetitive motivation; habituation to non-aversive stimuli	Appropriate species, strain; health status and history; duration of procedure; disruption of behavioral pattern of species; disruption of other coexisting species during field studies
B. Experiments on *unanesthetized* animals which may be expected to have no more than minimal pain and/or distress.	Procedures that are expected to be no more painful or distressful than administration of a medication or anesthetic agent: experiments involving minimal physical restraint related to physical examination, EEG, EKG, EMG in untrained animals; minimal deprivation; learning or conditioning with aversive stimulation of short duration or nontraumatic magnitude (e.g., mild shock, corneal air puff); injections/collections of blood samples or other body fluids; pain titration; dietary feeding; models of minimal disease; tumor growth not affecting normal function; product safety testing; short- and long-term studies of effects of chemical or other agents known not to have significant noxious, addicting, or intoxicating effects and measured noninvasively; pithing of frogs	As in Type A; duration of procedure; duration or restraint and/or deprivation; pithing should be carried out with the animal immobilized and wherever feasible at a temperature *no greater than* 40°F.

	Removal of tissue or organs for study	Method of euthanasia
C. Experimental use of animals after they have been painlessly killed.		
D. Acute experiments on *anesthetized* animals which will not be permitted to recover from anesthesia.	Physiological and neurophysiological studies; studies with chemical agents (e.g., CNS stimulants and depressants); nonsurvival surgical procedures	Mode and effectiveness of anesthesia; if neuromuscular (paralytic) agents are used in combination with anesthesia, appropriate personnel and equipment *must be available* to assure that the animal is ventilated and remains anesthetized.
E. Experimental procedures, including surgical procedures, carried out *under general or regional anesthesia* with intent of recovery. Recovery period with the animal's adaptation to the experimental intervention is considered an integral part of the experimental protocol, and no serious modifications to the animal's behavior, feeding, or ambulatory patterns are anticipated. No more than minimal to moderate pain and/or distress is anticipated which can be altered when necessary by the administration of appropriate analgesic and sedative drugs and proper veterinary care.	Biopsies, catheterizations, implantation of biomedical material, injection of substances to produce inflammatory reaction (e.g., lactic acid, colchicine); abdominal, thoracic or peripheral surgery (e.g., for implantation of chronic monitoring or support devices and for modification of internal organs); peripheral and central nervous system lesions and implants; pituitary removal; direct treatment, transfer, or sampling of fetuses or embryos in utero	As in Types A-D; appropriate facilities, aseptic technique and surgical procedures for the species involved; postoperative nursing care which also includes maintenance of body temperature, hydration, and control of pain and infection; duration of procedure; duration of postoperative pain and distress and consideration of use of analgesics; approval of full IACUC is necessary.
F. Experimental procedures, including surgical procedures as in E above, but where study is a progression of surgical or preoperative period and where surgical preparation may be a component of the overall study. The observation and study period after the intervention may produce more than moderate pain, distress, or illness and/or significantly impair the ability of the animal to function in its environment.	Shock; burn and organ transplant and rejection studies; severe trauma, extensive lesions or ablations	As in Type E and additional requirements for analgesia and sedation during remainder of procedure if necessary; approval of full IACUC is required.

TABLE 4-3 *Continued*

Types of Experiments	Examples of Procedures	Special Ethical Considerations
G. Experiments on *unanesthetized* animals which may be expected to have more than minimal pain and/or distress and/or where death is anticipated.	Administration of compounds resulting in damage to vital tissue or serious alteration of function; tests of drug efficacy to control severe pain; models of severe disease; severe trauma, injury, or shock; prolonged intense aversive stimulation; extensive tumor growth affecting normal function; studies which do not permit the animal to control the amount of intense painful stimuli it will receive or where drugs will not be administered to modify severe pain or distress; highly invasive studies of major sensory pathways; short- and long-term studies of the effects of chemical or other agents but known or expected to have significant noxious, addicting, or intoxicating effects	As in Type F and additional requirements for analgesia and sedation during remainder of procedure if necessary; specific justification is required to approve traumatic studies without proper anesthesia, analgesia, or sedation or with the nonsurgical use of neuromuscular (paralytic) agents without sedation or anesthesia; such studies must be conducted with special consideration for comfort of the animal and number of animals used; the investigator must specify the endpoint of the experiment as well as alternative situations in which termination of the experiment would be mandatory to avoid prolongation of suffering; such specification may be based on pathologic, physiologic, or behavioral observations; these procedures must not be carried out without approval of the full IACUC.

Similarities and Differences in Signs Among Humans and Animals

Humans often describe pain as sharp, dull, pricking, burning, or itching. Animals cannot relate such descriptions, so pain has to be assessed by observing their behavioral or physiologic reactions. Although many similarities between humans and animals can be used for pain detection (Vierck, 1976; Vierck et al., 1983; Zimmermann, 1984; Kitchell and Johnson, 1985), marked differences in pain tolerance must be kept in mind. The anthropomorphizing of pain perception should be tempered by the recognition of the many differences between humans and animals.

Pain thresholds are remarkably similar among all species and breeds of animals, but the perceived intensity and tolerance of pain vary among individual animals and in the same animal under different circumstances. Many factors—including strain, species, experience, age, health, and stress—affect pain tolerance (Wright et al., 1985; Breazile, 1987). Young animals might have a lower tolerance of acute pain than do older ones. A systemically ill animal might be less tolerant of pain than a healthy one, but a moribund or severely ill animal might be nonresponsive albeit in distress.

Some marked differences in pain responses between humans and animals are related to the site of pain. Abdominal surgery is thought to be less painful in four-legged animals than in humans, because humans use their abdominal muscles to a much greater extent in maintaining posture and for walking. A median sternotomy could be classified as producing low to moderate pain in humans and much pain in animals, probably because animals use their front limbs in walking and movement of sternal edges after the sternum has been surgically separated would be slight but painful during walking. A lateral thoracotomy is likely to be accompanied by less pain in animals than in humans, because respiration is more abdominal in animals and more thoracic in humans. Such differences account at least in part for the wide variety of signs seen in response to surgery (Soma, 1987).

Nonhuman Primates

Nonhuman primates show remarkably little reaction to surgical procedures or to injury, especially in the presence of humans, and might look well until they are gravely ill or in severe pain. Viewing an animal from a distance or by video could aid in detecting subtle clinical changes. Loud and persistent vocalization is an occasional but unreliable expression of pain; it is more likely to signify alarm or anger. Therefore, it should be recognized that a nonhuman primate that appears sick is likely to be critically ill and might require rapid attention. A nonhuman primate in pain has a general appearance of misery and dejection. It might huddle in a crouched posture with its arms across its chest and its head forward with a "sad" facial expression or a grimace and glassy eyes. It might moan or scream, avoid its companions, and stop grooming. A monkey in pain can also attract altered attention from its cagemates; this can vary from a lack of social grooming to attack. Acute abdominal pain can be shown by facial contortions, clenching of teeth, restlessness, and shaking accompanied by grunts and moans. Food and water are usually refused.

Dogs

Dogs in pain generally appear less alert and quieter than normal and have stiff body movements and an unwillingness to move. A dog in severe pain might lie still or adopt an abnormal posture to minimize its discomfort. In less severe pain, dogs can appear restless and more alert. There can be inappetence, shivering, and increased respiration with panting. Spontaneous barking is unlikely. They are more likely to whimper or howl, especially if unattended, and might growl without apparent provocation. Small breeds are generally more reactive to environmental changes than large dogs. Dogs can bite, scratch, or guard painful regions. When handled, they might be abnormally apprehensive or aggressive.

Cats

Cats are less reactive to environmental changes than dogs. A cat in pain is generally quiet and has an apprehensive facial expression, and its forehead might appear creased. It is inappetent and might cry, yowl, growl, or hiss if approached or made to move. It tends to hide or to separate itself from other cats. Its posture becomes stiff and abnormal, varying with the site of pain. If the pain is in its head or ears, it might tilt its head toward the affected side. A cat with generalized pain in both the thorax and abdomen might be crouched or hunched. If the pain is only thoracic, the head, neck, and body might be extended. A cat with abdominal or back pain might stand or lie on its side with its back arched or walk with a stilted gait. Incessant licking is sometimes associated with localized pain. Pain in one limb usually results in limping or holding up of the affected limb with no attempt to use it. Cats in severe or chronic pain look ungroomed and behave markedly differently from normal. Touching or palpation of a painful area might produce an immediate violent reaction and an attempt to escape. A general lack of well-being is an important indication of pain in cats.

Rabbits

Rabbits in pain can appear apprehensive, anxious, dull, or inactive and assume a hunched appearance, attempt to hide, and squeal or cry. But sometimes they show aggressive behavior with increased activity and excessive scratching and licking. Reactions to handling are exaggerated, and acute pain might result in vocalization. With abdominal pain, they sometimes grind their teeth and salivate excessively. Their respiratory rate can be increased, and they can be inappetent.

Rabbits in distress might cannibalize their young and tend to be more susceptible to the tonic immobility reflex, a phenomenon that is thought to block pain in prey species (see Chapter 5).

Laboratory Rodents

Pain in rodents usually results in decreased activity, piloerection, and an ungroomed appearance. There can be excessive licking and scratching, which can progress to self-mutilation. They might adopt an abnormal stance or a hunched posture. Respiration can be rapid and shallow with grunting or chattering on expiration. Pupils might be dilated. In albinos, porphyrin secretion ("red tears") can be seen around the eyes and nose.

Rats and mice in acute pain might vocalize and become unusually aggressive when handled. Their squeal can be at an unusually high pitch or at a frequency above human hearing. Inappetence or a change in feeding activity can be noted. They might eat bedding or their offspring. If they are housed with others, the normal group behavior or grooming might change. They might separate from the rest of the animals in the cage and attempt to hide.

Normal guinea pigs will stampede and squeal when frightened, when attempts are made to handle them, or when strangers are in the room, but sick guinea pigs and those in pain will usually remain quiet. Other behaviors of guinea pigs in pain are similar to those of rats and mice.

Horses

Horses in acute pain show reluctance to be handled, and their other responses are varied: periods of restlessness, interrupted feeding with food held in the mouth uneaten, anxious appearance with dilated pupils and glassy eyes, increased respiration and pulse rate with flared nostrils, profuse sweating, and a rigid stance. In prolonged pain, their behavior might change from restlessness to depression with head lowered. In pain associated with skeletal damage, there is reluctance to move; limbs might be held in unusual positions, and the head and neck in a fixed position. Horses with abdominal pain might look at, bite, or kick their abdomen; get up and lie down frequently; walk in circles; and sweat, roll, and injure themselves as a result of these activities, with bruising especially around the eyes. That state can progress and last for several hours. When near collapse, they might quietly stand rigid and unmoving, but with signs of deteriorating circulatory status, such as mucosal cyanosis and prolonged capillary filling time.

Cattle

Cattle in pain often appear dull and depressed, hold their heads low, and show little interest in their surroundings. There is inappetence, weight loss, and, in milking cows, a sudden decrease in milk yield. Severe pain often results in rapid, shallow respiration. On handling, they might react violently or adopt a rigid posture designed to immobilize the painful region. Grunting and grinding of teeth might be heard. Localized pain might be associated with persistent licking or kicking at the offending area and, when the pain is severe, with bellowing. Generally, signs of abdominal pain are similar to those in horses, but less marked. Rigid posture can lead to a lack of grooming because of an unwillingness to turn the neck. In acute abdominal conditions, such as intestinal strangulation, cattle adopt a characteristic stance with one hind foot placed directly in front of the other.

Sheep and Goats

In general, signs of pain in sheep and goats are similar to those in cattle, but sheep, in particular, tolerate severe injury without overt signs of pain or distress. Changes in posture and movement are often apparent, and a change in facial expression might be observed. There is a general reluctance to move. Goats are more likely than cattle to vocalize in response to pain. Grinding of teeth and grunting are also heard. After castration or tail docking, lambs might show signs of pain by standing and lying repeatedly, wagging their tails, occasionally bleating, and displaying neck extension, dorsal lip curling, kicking, rolling, and hyperventilation.

Pigs

Pigs in pain might show changes in social behavior, gait, and posture and an absence of bed-making. Pigs normally squeal and attempt to escape when handled, and pain can accentuate these reactions. Adults might become aggressive. Squealing is also characteristic when painful areas are palpated. Pigs in pain often are unwilling to move and might hide in bedding if possible.

Birds

Birds in pain can show escape reactions, vocalization, and excessive movement. Small species struggle less and emit fewer distress calls than large species. Head movements increase in extent and frequency. There can be an increase in heart and respiratory rates. Prolonged pain results in inappetence, inactivity, and a drooping, miserable appearance. The eyes might be partially closed, the wings held flat against the body, and the neck retracted. When a bird is handled, its escape reaction might be replaced by tonic immobility (see Chapter 5). Birds with limb pain avoid use of the affected limb and "guard" it from extension.

Reptiles

Acute pain in reptiles can be characterized by flinching and muscle contractions. There might be aversive movements away from the unpleasant stimulus and attempts to bite. More chronic and persistent pain might be associated with anorexia, lethargy, and weight loss, although it is difficult to associate any of these signs of lack of well-being specifically with pain.

Fish

It is difficult to determine the nature of the response to pain in fish, and we cannot tell whether the experience is similar to that in mammals (Arena and Richardson, 1990). Fish exhibit a pronounced initial response to injuries or to contact with irritants, but their response to chronic stimuli might be small or absent. Fish with severe wounds, which would cause immobility in a mammal, often appear to behave normally and even resume feeding. Fish react to noxious stimuli, such as puncture with a hypodermic needle, with strong muscular movements. When exposed to a noxious environment, such as an acidic solution, they show abnormal swimming behavior and attempt to jump from the water, their coloring becomes darker, and their opercular movements become more rapid. Such effects indicate some, perhaps considerable, distress, but it is not possible to describe the distress unequivocally as pain-induced.

RECOGNITION AND ASSESSMENT OF STRESS AND DISTRESS

The most potent sources of stress in captive environments, other than pain, are likely to fall within the six ecologic dimensions described in Chapter 3; some of the most common are summarized in Table 4-4. Some useful information for a given species on conditions in the captive environment that are likely to be stressful can be gleaned from descriptions of the behavior of the species in its natural habitat, but such information is no substitute for data based on experiments carefully conducted in the captive environment.

In assessing stress and distress in an animal, one should first determine whether the source is pain (acute or chronic) or other factors. That might be evident from the animal's recent history. If the animal is in pain, it might also be in distress. Or some unrelated, nonpain stressor could be producing distress or potentiating the pain. If it is determined that a stressor other than pain is contributing to the animal's distress, its nature and source should be determined (Chapter 3). Distress caused by pain alone generally abates when the pain is relieved. But non-pain-induced distress should be addressed as a problem separate and distinct from pain and usually requires a nonpharmacologic (environmental) approach.

As indicated earlier, stress and distress are complex syndromes that are difficult to define and even harder to interpret and recognize (Wright et al., 1985). The recognition and assessment of stress and distress and the identification of events that induce them present many problems not often apparent to the untrained observer (Crane, 1987). The syndromes are among the physiologically most complex and psychologically compelling experiences that a human, and presum-

TABLE 4-4   Potential Causes of Stress in Laboratory Animals[a]

Husbandry Practices
  • Inappropriate or variable temperature, humidity, ventilation, or illumination
  • Inappropriate cage or enclosure size
  • Noise
  • Too infrequent change in bedding or removal of waste
  • Stale food or dirty water
  • Denial of positive social stimulation
  • Maternal deprivation
  • Social intimidation or abuse by companions
  • Unprofessional behaviors or practices

Experimental Design
  • Food and water deprivation
  • Inadequate caging
  • Poor or inappropriate technique
  • Failure to adapt or handle animals
  • Restraint
  • Social deprivation
  • Frequent changes in procedures or personnel

---

[a]This table is not meant to be all-inclusive and excludes situations in which pain-induced stress can arise (e.g., postsurgical recovery). It is assumed that animals are otherwise physically healthy.

ably an animal, can have. It is important that we develop the ability to recognize and deal with them in animals (Steffey, 1983). Just how a particular species will respond and cope with stimuli that can induce stress is difficult to predict. There can be a great deal of interspecies and individual variability, so one animal might respond quite differently from another (Vierck, 1976). That variability can be decreased in some common laboratory animals, such as mice and rats, in which generations of breeding have tended to produce animals that respond to stressful stimuli relatively uniformly (Hughes and Lang, 1983). But variability is accentuated in highly outbred populations, such as dogs and cats, or in such a highly diverse order as nonhuman primates. Some breeds of dogs, such as hounds, are noted for their hardiness and stoic demeanor and might be less likely to show stress in response to the same stimuli that cause sharp reactions in other breeds, such as toy poodles.

DIAGNOSIS OF STRESS AND DISTRESS

The following discussion approaches the diagnosis of pain-induced and non-pain-induced stress and distress from a problem-oriented perspective. Table 4-5 lists common behaviors and physiologic and biochemical characteristics, changes in which can indicate stress or changes in well-being.

Assessing an Animal's Records

The first direct information about an animal should be readily apparent from examination of its cage card and clinical record. This information should include species and breed, date the animal was received, genetic origin and vendor, age, sex, population density in the cage, previous experimentation or illness, and reproductive activity or status (Spinelli and Markowitz, 1987). Surgical procedures—including the use of anesthetics and analgesics and presurgical and postsurgical care—should be included in the record. Food intake should be examined, not only for amount, but for pattern of feeding or waste. Waste of food or failure to eat can indicate illness, spilling, lack of palatability, spoiling, or oral lesions.

Assessing the Environment

A scheme should be developed for assessing each animal in a logical, organized fashion. Initial assessment should be carried out at a distance (Morton and Griffiths, 1985; Wright et al., 1985). The animal should be observed for its appearance and behavior before it is disturbed. On entry into the animal room, the assessor should be aware of the animal's environment. The room temperature, humidity, ventilation, odors, and indication of contamination by vermin should all be considered. A well-trained clinician or technician can often "feel" abnormal environmental situations. If the assessor is unsure about the animal's well-being, expert advice should be sought.

TABLE 4-5 Some Behavioral, Physiologic, and Biochemical Indicators of Well-Being

Behavioral	Physiologic	Biochemical
Grooming	Temperature	Corticosteroids
Appetite	Pulse	Catecholamines
Activity	Respiration	Thyroxin
Aggression	Weight loss	Prolactin
Facial expression	Blood-cell count	β-Endorphin
Vocalization	Blood-cell structure	ACTH
Appearance	Cardiac output	Glucagon
Posture	Blood flow	Insulin
Response to handling		Vasopressin
		Substance P

[a]Departures from normal behaviors and characteristics are suggestive of changes in well-being. A knowledge of species-typical and individual-specific behaviors and clinical values is essential.

Stress and Distress Caused by Lack of Environmental Stimuli

Most attention to animal stress focuses on techniques that involve obviously aversive stimuli. In human medicine, however, it is known that lack of external stimuli can cause psychiatric disorders. Researchers have demonstrated that laboratory animals sometimes develop severe signs of distress from a lack of essential stimulation. (This topic is discussed in greater detail in Chapter 3.) The recent focus on the "psychologic well-being" of nonhuman primates has raised the issue repeatedly, and many have proposed to improve psychologic well-being with enrichment devices or programs. Although nonhuman primates have received nearly all the attention, it should be asked whether other laboratory animals are in distress as a result of environmental monotony in standard housing or lack of other unidentified components of the environment. Understimulated animals of many species show abnormal behavior patterns (stereotypes and displacement behaviors) that are largely absent in enriched environments (Wemelsfelder, 1990). Animals in unenriched environments are also more passive, and their behaviors might be less diverse than those of animals in more stimulating surroundings.

Assessing a Species and an Individual Animal

When stress is present, the first change most likely to be reported is a change in an animal's activity pattern. Behavior can range from inactivity to hyperactivity and from adaptive to maladaptive, depending on the source and severity of the stressor and the species. Changes can be seen in sleep and eating behavior. The animal might be nonresponsive, listless, lethargic, and depressed, or it might be unusually restless, excitable, anxious, apprehensive, hypersensitive, or aggressive. It might constantly move about the enclosure or repeatedly stand and lie down. As one approaches a normal animal's cage, it should respond in a usual and predictable manner that enables assessment of its gait, inquisitiveness, vocalization, and posture. An animal in stress that previously would have investigated a new visitor to the room or a change in the environment might now fail to do so or attempt to escape.

Nocturnal species, which during daylight hours exhibit very little species-typical behavior other than sleeping, should be observed at times that coincide with their active period, e.g., early in the morning, when the animals are still awake and moving about. During initial observations, respiratory and activity patterns should be assessed without investigator-produced stimulation or the escape behaviors that are often associated with capturing and handling.

Assessing Behavior

The definition and measurement of distress are in their infancy. Few attempts have been made to place the assessment of distress on a scientific and systematic basis. The transition between *atypical* behaviors expressed as a homeostatic process of adapting to stress and the *maladaptive* behaviors expressed as distress might not always be clearly defined. Atypical behaviors can be developed by an animal to cope with the constraints of a laboratory environment or experimental conditions and might indicate that it is in acute stress. However, assessment of the meaning of an atypical behavior requires the most diligent attention and professional judgment. Although an animal that shows such behavior is not necessarily in distress, the potential transition period between acute stress and distress should be of concern to investigators and animal staffs. The duration of atypical behaviors and the type of behaviors involved should constitute a warning that an animal needs attention; serious attempts must be made to alleviate the potential for distress. Distinctive species-typical responses to pain and to fear are shown by many species and are usually easy to recognize. A limitation on the use of these species-typical indicators is that the conditions that elicit pain and fear make up a relatively narrow and specific subset of the total range of captivity situations that are likely to cause distress.

A situation in which an animal is unable to perform all the normal or instinctive behaviors of its species should not always be considered as causing stress or even distress. As a blanket prescription, this has obvious shortcomings. The assumption is that a monkey that never screams in fear, a hen that is unable to dust bathe, a cat that is unable to capture live prey, or a rabbit or rat that is unable to burrow is distressed. The committee believes that an expression of species-typical behavior is preferable, but that a state of well-being can exist even if species-typical behaviors are not all manifest. There is no evidence that all normal activities of a species are based on specific behavioral needs or motives whose blocking causes distress.

As indicated in Chapters 1 and 3, an animal that shows behaviors that are abnormal or atypical for its species should not always be considered distressed. To be sure, some behaviors are clearly contrary to well-being and are undesirable on that basis alone; self-mutilation is an example. But animals might develop other atypical behaviors to cope with the constraints of their captive environment or to take advantage of the special opportunities it provides. Rather than being signs of distress, some atypical behaviors could be ways of adapting to stress and reducing or controlling distress.

Another approach to the assessment of distress is based on the reasonable assumption that situations that act as rewards or provide positive reinforcement are pleasant for an animal, and situations that it will work to avoid are unpleasant or distressful (Dawkins, 1976, 1983). Dawkins (1990) suggests that distress occurs in situations in which captive animals "are prevented from doing something they are highly motivated to do."

No criterion or method for the assessment of distress is without value, and none is free of limitations. The presence or absence of species-typical behaviors should certainly be considered, although it is not sufficient for evaluating distress. Maladaptive behavior is important, but should be interpreted cautiously. Behavioral methods for measuring motivation, such as those proposed by Dawkins, have been available for many years and can play an important role in the assessment of distress, but they are not without problems. No measure of motivation provides an adequate index of its "strength" (e.g., Miller, 1956). *Motivation*, like *stress*, does not refer to a unitary process or single "drive" (e.g., Fentress, 1973; Mason and Capitanio, 1988). Furthermore, the relationship between the strength of motivational "demand" and distress is not obvious. It is at least conceivable that an animal can be highly motivated to achieve a particular "commodity" and yet show no signs of distress or other untoward effects when this commodity is not available.

Behavioral changes, however, are the earliest signs of stress or distress that most animal care staff and researchers are likely to confront. Skilled observers who know the behavior of a particular species or strain of animal and of the individual animals under their care could provide a reliable assessment of the state of the animals. That reliability is seriously compromised when few animal care staff and researchers are afforded the time or training necessary for them to become skilled observers.

Barclay et al. (1988) argue that departures from normal behavior in rats and mice can be produced by relatively minor procedures, but that some behaviors—such as feeding, drinking, and sleeping—have too high a priority to the animal to be used as baseline indexes for relatively minor stress, because they are not easily perturbed. Barclay et al. assume, from analogy and intuition, that change in behavior is related directly to severity of pain and stress. Whether or not that is true, a change in behavior should alert human observers. For example, Antin et al. (1975) report that rats engage in a specific and predictable pattern of postprandial grooming behavior; a persistent change in this pattern clearly suggests that something is amiss that involves the animal's well-being.

PHYSIOLOGIC AND BIOCHEMICAL INDICATORS OF PAIN AND STRESS

Although it used to be thought that the response to stress was an invariant physiologic reaction, recent studies support the idea that the stress response is not invariant, but depends on an integrated activation of various neural and endocrine factors. A variety of physiologic and biochemical characteristics change when an animal is in pain, stress, or distress (Dawkins, 1990), although many also change with the onset of general arousal, as in play or sexual excitement (see also Chapter 3). The relative importance of those factors depends on the type of stressor—physical (e.g., tissue damage or immobilization), physiologic (e.g., exercise), or psychologic (e.g., altered environment)—and on its magnitude, frequency, and timing. An animal can either habituate and adapt to a chronic stressor or develop maladaptive behavior that leads to distress. Regardless of whether the animal has habituated to a chronic stressor or shows maladaptive behavior, additional novel stimuli can evoke or increase the intensity of a stress response. Other factors that can influence the stress response include age, sex, physical fitness, experience, disease, and medication.

Neural and endocrine substances are released in response to a stressor and play an important role in the initiation and coordination of the behavioral, cardiovascular, and immunologic responses to stress. The site of origin of those substances influences the physiologic stress response, which has two categories of duration: a rapid increase in circulating neurally derived substances with a short duration of action and a slower increase in endocrine-derived substances with a longer duration of action.

Acute stress—surgery, postoperative pain, burns, anesthesia, cardiac arrest, exercise, and sometimes headache—results in the hypothalamic secretion of corticotropin-releasing factor (CRF). CRF then stimulates the pituitary to cosecrete adrenocorticotropic hormone (ACTH), which promptly stimulates the release of corticosteroids from the adrenal cortex and the opioid peptides ß-lipotropin and ß-endorphin. In humans, plasma concentrations of these hormones can increase by a factor of 2-5 during stress. The roles of ß-lipotropin and ß-endorphin in the stress response are poorly understood. ß-Endorphin might play a role in pain modulation (Hargreaves et al., 1983, 1987; Pickar et al., 1983; Szyfelbein et al., 1985). A potential target of circulating ß-endorphin could be inflamed tissue (Joris et al., 1987).

The major example of neurally derived responses to acute stress is the activation of the sympathoadrenal system. The pituitary-adrenal axis responds with a prompt increase in catecholamines from the adrenal medulla, which is usually followed by an increase in corticosteroids. Plasma concentrations of catecholamines increase considerably after surgery or postoperative pain, because of increased circulating concentrations of epinephrine, primarily from the adrenal medulla, and norepinephrine, primarily from sympathetic nerve terminal activation (Goldstein, 1987). Those different components of the sympathoadrenal system can be regulated separately. The sympathoneural release of norepinephrine evokes a regionally selective effect, whereas the adrenal medulla produces an increase in systemic plasma concentrations of epinephrine. The physiologic consequences of activation of those systems include increased cardiac output, increased skeletal muscle blood flow, cutaneous vasoconstriction, reduced gut motility, and increased glucose availability.

Hormonally derived responses to stress result from changes in concentrations of growth hormone, prolactin, glucagon, insulin, vasopressin, neuropeptides, and other hormones. Acute stress causes increased secretion of growth hormone and prolactin, both from the anterior pituitary. Prolactin participates in metabolic processes and might modify nociception, but concentrations remain in the normal range in the presence of chronic stress. The significance of the short-lasting growth hormone increase is not known. Glucagon increases in response to acute stress, and insulin decreases. The decrease in insulin—in combination with increased prolactin, growth hormone, glucagon, and epinephrine—contributes to the development of hyperglycemia.

Surgery, burns, and migraine headaches in people can evoke vasopressin release from nerve endings in the posterior pituitary. Circulating vasopressin can influence vascular tone and diuresis and might also modulate nociception (Berson et al., 1983). Surgical trauma leads to increases in circulating neuropeptides, such as substance P and calcitonin gene-related peptide, possibly from unmyelinated nerve fibers activated at the site of inflammation and injury. Those neuropeptides are important in plasma extravasation and in the release of histamine from mast cells and serotonin from platelets. Their physiologic role after circulation in plasma is unknown.

Responses to persistent stressors, such as chronic stress or distress, are more variable than responses to acute stress; catecholamines might return to normal values, and corticosteroid concentrations might be increased, unchanged, or decreased. Thus, changes in concentrations of pituitary and adrenal hormones can be used as markers of acute stress, but their usefulness in the recognition of chronic stress or distress is questionable at best.

Biochemical markers are not unequivocal indicators of either pain or distress, but, when used in conjunction with behavioral and environmental data, they can reinforce a diagnosis. An acute stressor can produce a transient but important change in some characteristics; a chronic stressor can lead to the establishment of a new steady state of plasma hormones and heart function that might not be very different from the original. Different animals can respond to a given event differently, sometimes because of a lack of opportunity to habituate or acclimate. Care should be exercised when the effects of stress or distress could interfere with experimental results, because laboratory facilities and husbandry procedures can have different effects on individual animals.

PHARMACOLOGIC ASSESSMENT OF DISTRESS

It is not always possible to use behavioral or physiologic measures to distinguish between pain-induced distress and distress induced by other stimuli, but the use of pharmacologic techniques offers some interesting options in this regard. If an animal's behavior returns to normal after the administration of an analgesic, but not after administration of an anxiolytic, one would be justified in concluding that the distress was caused by a painful stimulus. One could similarly find that the distress was induced by fear or anxiety, rather than pain.

Other drug-based approaches that raise some intriguing questions about animal distress include the recent investigations of the effects of opioid receptor antagonists on stereotypic behaviors in animals. Stereotypic behavior in a confined animal is sometimes considered to be a sign of distress. It is interesting that antagonists reduce or eliminate bar-chewing in confined pigs, crib-biting in stabled horses, and lick granulomas in dogs (Cronin et al., 1986; Dodman et al., 1987; White, 1990).

5

Control of Pain

The goal of this chapter is to provide guidance to investigators and veterinarians in the selection of suitable pharmacologic agents and management strategies for the prevention or alleviation of pain in laboratory animals. The first section provides a rational basis for the pharmacologic control of pain. It discusses the pharmacology of general anesthesia in laboratory animals and describes the major classes of drugs used to achieve the clinical goals of analgesia, sedation, and restraint (see Table 5-1). Discussion of the major drug classes is organized for the reader to extract information along three dimensions—clinical use, pharmacologic effects, and dose recommendations—each related to particular species. The second part addresses the nonpharmacologic control of pain and deals with the use of hypothermia, tonic immobility, and acupuncture.

The first part of this chapter focuses on experimental paradigms in which pain is an integral part of the study, but the concepts presented should also be considered applicable to pain of clinical, surgical, or inapparent sources.

An important idea regarding laboratory animals in pain involves an anthropomorphic analogy that animals should not be exposed to pain greater than human beings would tolerate (Bowd, 1980) and that, "unless the contrary is established, investigators should consider that procedures that cause pain and distress in human beings may cause pain or distress in other animals" (IRAC, 1985). Human subjects in pain studies are exposed only to painful stimuli that they will tolerate, and they can remove a painful stimulus at any time. Low levels of pain (near the pain threshold) induce minimal discomfort and stress and are well tolerated by animals or human subjects. Most human pain is of this type, and it is part of our daily experience. Only when pain becomes severe (approaching pain tolerance levels) is our behavior dominated by attempts to avoid or escape it. That degree of pain needs to be alleviated. In pain studies, giving animals control over the source of pain is an effective way to let them minimize it. In that situation, escape-avoidance behavior is an appropriate adaptive response. An animal displaying such behavior might be experiencing discomfort, but is not yet in distress (see Table 1-3). However, if the animal is denied control of the stimulus and it approaches or exceeds the limit of tolerance, maladaptive behaviors will appear and the animal should be considered to be in distress. In distressed animals, maladaptive behaviors can include persistent attacks on the perceived source of the pain (e.g., electrified grid floors or other parts of the apparatus), prolonged immobilization or "freezing," self-mutilation of the area of the body receiving the stimulus, or a state of learned helplessness in which the animal gives up and no longer attempts to escape, avoid, or control the stimulus.

In most experiments involving the study of pain, the animal or the investigator can set a limit on the magnitude and duration of the stimulus. The investigator must determine the intensity and duration of the pain that the animal experiences and minimize it.

Four general approaches are available to minimize pain (Dubner, 1987): use of general anesthesia or neurosurgery, use of local anesthesia and analgesia, training of animals to control the stimulus, and control of the stimulus by the investigator.

When an invasive procedure is performed on an appropriately anesthetized animal, there is little concern about pain as long as the animal remains anesthetized. The anesthetic state can be monitored by assessing pupillary size, palpebral and toe-pinch response, stability of heart rate and blood pressure, and electroencephalographic activity. In a study in which anesthetic agents would confound the data, surgical lesions of the central nervous system can be made under anesthesia, the animal allowed to recover from anesthesia, and data collected on a functional decerebrate with no possibility of conscious* sensation. An alternative to anesthesia or neurosurgery in some studies, and often a valuable adjunct to anesthesia, is the administration of local anesthetic or analgesic agents to eliminate or reduce pain.

Some studies are concerned with pain mechanisms and the relationship between pain-related behavior and neurobiologic processes and require that animals be exposed to actual or potential tissue damage. In others, pain might be a consequence of techniques and methods whose purposes are unrelated to the nature or magnitude of the pain produced. In most such investigations with conscious animals, the animals can be taught to avoid or escape painful stimuli.

An important distinction should be made between reflexes associated with nociception and the maladaptive behaviors associated with distress when pain

---

*The terms *conscious* and *consciousness* are used throughout this text to refer to the awake state, the state in which stimuli can be perceived (e.g., "The conscious animal is aware of its surroundings"). *Unconsciousness* refers to the state in which stimuli are not perceived (e.g., "The anesthetic should produce a loss of consciousness").

exceeds the limit of tolerance. A nociceptive reflex can occur without the perception of pain. In studies in which animals experience pain, methods that allow them to control the intensity and duration of pain include withdrawal responses elicited by stimulating their paws or tails so that they move their paws or tails away from the source of aversive stimulation (Dubner, 1987). In tasks that use such reflexive measures, animals often need to be placed under considerable restraint, and that might produce stress that can influence the outcome of an experiment (Gärtner et al., 1980; Pare and Glavin, 1986). Such stress is minimized by the use of unrestrained escape-avoidance tasks, in which animals are taught to control the stimulus. The teaching uses operant-conditioning procedures and closely mimics conditions under which humans participate in experimental pain studies: animals choose to participate by initiating trials (e.g., to obtain food), they determine the magnitudes of aversive stimulation that they will accept by refusing to obtain food and escaping intolerable stimuli, and they can withdraw from the experiment by ceasing to initiate new trials.

The most difficult types of experiments in which pain should be minimized include those in which animals cannot control the magnitude of the painful stimulus. In such experiments, the investigator or veterinarian must assess the pain (see Chapter 4). That should be done first by knowledgeable assessment of the intensity of the stimulus and second, when possible, by having the investigator receive the maximal stimulus that it is possible to deliver to the animal in the protocol being used. The committee believes that that practice can yield a useful estimate of stimulus potency. Others believe that so little might be known about the stimulus characteristics that it would be difficult to know what to match when the same stimulus is applied to another animal; if this is the case, it can lead to an underestimation of the pain that a given animal might experience.

Whenever an animal is in an experimental situation and after its return to its home cage, its behavior should be carefully monitored. While it is in an experimental trial, does it attack the experimental apparatus or parts of its own body? Does it control the stimulus through smoothly coordinated behaviors? When returned to its home cage, does it have an abnormal gait and appear unusually aggressive? Does it look at or groom the injured area excessively? Does it have an unusual posture and guard an injured limb excessively? Does it have normal food and water intake and maintain its body weight in comparison with control animals? Does it exhibit normal social adjustment when placed in a cage with other animals of the same species and respond normally to its handler? Is its sleeping-waking cycle normal? Does it exhibit abnormal vocalization, such as whimpering or crying? Has its species-typical behavior changed? Questions like those underlie the importance of knowing the normal behavioral characteristics of a particular species and the intensity of aversive stimuli. Although the answer to any one of the above questions alone does not necessarily indicate that an animal is in pain or distress, the presence of changes in several elements of behavior does suggest that pain is intolerable. The experimenter and a veterinarian should determine whether the pain can be reduced and whether the experiment can be performed with less pain.

PHARMACOLOGIC CONTROL OF PAIN

In studies in which pain is not the focus, pharmacologic control of pain is usually required. The use of drugs requires consideration of several interacting factors (Short and Van Poznak, 1992).

• What is the clinical goal of drug administration? Common clinical goals include general anesthesia for surgical procedures, lighter general anesthesia for experimental studies that cannot be conducted in awake animals, sedation and analgesia for minor surgical and diagnostic procedures, management of postsurgical pain and pain associated with disease, sedation and tranquilization for the relief of non-pain-induced stress or distress, and temporary restraint.

• What are the pharmacologic actions of the drugs being considered? That is important if they will be used before an experimental study. Knowledge of the pharmacology, pharmacodynamics, duration of action, species-typical actions, and specific actions on the organ systems under study is important for proper interpretation of experimental data. Drugs that are least likely to influence the systems under study should be chosen. Pain and pain-induced distress can be adequately alleviated pharmacologically, but drug actions often confound interpretation of experimental results, because every drug has actions in addition to the one for which it is used (e.g., pain relief). Nevertheless, pharmacologic management is efficacious, often necessary, and usually experimentally acceptable. Knowledge of the so-called side-effects of drugs, however, is important both to the well-being of animals and to an understanding of their potential contributions to experimental outcomes.

• How do species vary in their responses to the drugs being considered, and how are responses affected by other factors? Actions and doses in one animal species might not be relevant in another species. Not only do dosages vary by species, breed, and strain, but other factors—such as sex, environment, age, nutrition, and health status—play a major role; the very young, old, or obese present a greater anesthetic challenge. For example, male mice sleep longer than female mice after the administration of pentobarbital. Environmental factors have been shown to affect hepatic drug-metabolizing enzyme systems (microsomal liver enzymes). Softwood bedding, such as pine or cedar, contains aromatic amines that induce the hepatic microsomal enzymes, thereby increasing barbiturate metabolism and reducing sleeping time. In contrast, hardwood bedding or the absence of bedding (as in the use of wire-bottom cages) allows hepatic enzymes to remain at a resting state, so sleeping times might be longer. A dirty environment might inhibit drug-metabolizing enzymes and thus prolong anesthesia. Anesthetics given repeatedly at short intervals can induce hepatic microsomes and thus increase anesthetic metabolism and decrease sleeping time. Fasting is important especially in herbivorous species, in which ingesta can account for a substantial portion of an animal's body weight; the gastrointestinal tracts of herbivores are not empty after a 24-hour fast.

Drugs categorized as general anesthetics, sedatives, hypnotics, ataractics, anxiolytics, tranquilizers, nonsteroidal anti-inflammatory drugs, and opioids all have been used to prevent or minimize pain and distress produced by painful and nonpainful procedures and to produce unconsciousness and analgesia for surgical procedures. Barbiturates and inhalational anesthetics are considered general anesthetics and are commonly used as total anesthetic agents, that is, drugs that produce unconsciousness and muscle relaxation sufficient for surgical intervention. Barbiturates are also considered hypnotics and are used in veterinary medicine as general anesthetics.

General anesthetics produce a total loss of awareness and of responsiveness to painful stimuli during surgical procedures. Other drugs are also used to alleviate pain and distress. Neuroleptanalgesics, dissociative anesthetics, and continuously infused potent opioids in people or animals premedicated with low doses of hypnotics or benzodiazepines are used for producing surgical anesthesia. Opioids are used because of their cardiovascular-sparing aspects and lack of profound depression of the central nervous system (CNS); they should therefore be considered for studies involving the CNS and cardiovascular system.

The opioid agonists, which include the morphine-like drugs (e.g., fentanyl and oxymorphone), produce analgesia and sedation through the activation of opioid receptors in the CNS. The dissociative anesthetic agent ketamine has both analgesic and anesthetic properties, but should be combined with other drugs for major procedures. The anti-inflammatory action of the nonsteroidal anti-inflammatory drugs is a major factor in their analgesic effects.

It should be emphasized that many of the drugs to be discussed here, with the exception of the opioids, are CNS depressants and might not be good analgesics. Tranquilizers, ataractics, and hypnotics can be used as adjuncts in the treatment of non-pain-induced stress and distress, but *not* for the treatment of pain. Many combinations of drugs have been used in various species for analgesia, sedation, restraint, and general anesthesia. Table 5-1 shows clinical uses of drugs in various classes included in this chapter.

GENERAL ANESTHESIA

The aim of general anesthesia is to produce unconsciousness as rapidly and as smoothly as possible and to maintain a depth of anesthesia appropriate for the objectives of the surgery or study. The depth of anesthesia might have to be varied on the basis of the intensity of the stimulation and changing physiologic conditions, as the anesthetist attempts to balance adequate anesthesia and analgesia with physiologic function. The level of anesthesia required can vary from moderate for surgical intervention to light for the study period that follows. Considerable information is available on the pharmacologic effects of anesthetic agents on organ functions in some species (Merin, 1975; Covino et al., 1985; Miller, 1990). General anesthesia can affect all physiologic functions; for inhalational anesthetics, the magnitude of the affects is related to the alveolar concentration of the specific drug.

TABLE 5-1 Use of Drugs

Category	Analgesia	Anxiolysis	Sedation	Anesthesia
Inhalational anesthetic	—	—	—	PA
Barbiturates	—	PA	PA	PA
Cyclohexamines	PA	—	—	PA
Neuroleptanalgesics	PA	—	PA	SA-C
Benzodiazepines	—	PA	—	C
Tranquilizers	—	PA	PA	C
Opioid agonists	PA	—	PA	C
Opioid agonist-antagonists	PA	—	SA	—
Nonsteroidal anti-inflammatory drugs	PA	—	—	—

NOTE: PA = primary action; SA = secondary action; C = combined with other drugs.

Research animals undergoing general anesthesia differ somewhat from animals normally encountered in clinical veterinary practice. Research animals usually are not ill or traumatized and generally are of the same species as the other animals within the study and have similar characteristics. Once a research model has been selected, consistency between animals is very important. Whether recovery and postoperative care are part of the experimental protocol or recovery is not intended, the concern for the management of anesthesia and care during the procedures should be identical, because it should be assumed that general anesthesia will affect whatever system is under study. The investigator should perturb the organ system under study only during a steady state of anesthesia (Soma and Klide, 1987; Soma et al., 1988a); this minimizes the effect of changing depths of anesthesia on the animal and allows interpretation of data from the standpoint of a known, established baseline. Data from different laboratories often are not easily compared, and differences in methods of anesthesia can contribute to the difficulty. Ultimate goals of clinical and investigative anesthesia might differ, but the basic principles of good anesthetic techniques do not: maintain a depth of anesthesia that minimizes changes in physiologic function, blocks response to stimulation, and produces unconsciousness.

Inhalational Anesthesia

The development of inhalational anesthesia for both companion and laboratory animals has progressed a great deal in the last 20 years. It is beyond the scope of this section to describe the various methods and equipment that can be used for the administration of inhalational anesthesia to a broad range of animals, but information is readily available (Soma, 1971; Lumb and Jones, 1984; Hartsfield, 1987; Klide, 1989). Inhalational anesthesia can be administered by mask for a short procedure in most animals, but for longer periods of anesthesia the trachea should be intubated for better control of the airway and depth of anesthesia. The ease of tracheal intubation varies from difficult in rodents and ruminants to easy in carnivores (Lumb and Jones, 1984; Short, 1987).

The advantages of inhalational anesthesia for both the preparative and study periods include the ability to define and vary the depth of anesthesia and estimate the alveolar concentration. The end-tidal alveolar concentration of an anesthetic at which 50% of animals (ED_{50}) will not respond to a specified painful stimulus is the minimal alveolar concentration (MAC) (Eger et al., 1965; Eger, 1978) (Table 5-2). At 1.0 MAC, animals are unconscious and under anesthesia, but 50% will respond to a noxious stimulus. Adequate surgical anesthesia occurs between 1.25 and 1.50 MAC, and 1.3 MAC is considered the ED_{95}. At 0.4 MAC, humans can respond to verbal commands (Stoelting et al., 1970). The MAC in some animals is slightly higher than that measured in humans (White et al., 1974; Steffey et al., 1977; Eger, 1978; Weiskopf and Bogetz, 1984); this could be a real species difference or could be due to the use of different measurement criteria. Despite some differences, the MAC is roughly consistent between species. It must be emphasized that the MAC represents alveolar concentration and that it is measured as end-tidal concentration. The MAC is agent-specific and can be used to establish a consistent depth of anesthesia and to compare agents.

The MAC also defines the potency of inhalational agents; the lower the MAC, the more potent the anesthetic. The selection, measurement, and maintenance of the end-tidal concentration at some multiple of the MAC will allow light anesthesia to be used with neuromuscular blocking agents while ensuring an adequate depth of anesthesia. Under these circumstances, the investigator can be confident that the animal is unconscious. The MAC can be used to establish a consistent depth of anesthesia during a study and between animals. The establishment of the MAC for a study ensures that changes in physiologic functions are fairly consistent and are not due to changes in the depth of anesthesia.

TABLE 5-2   MAC Values of Anesthetics in Different Species (% End-Tidal Alveolar Concentration)[a]

Agent	Dog	Human	Cat	Rat or Mouse	Goldfish	Toad	Horse	Swine
Enflurane	2.20	1.68	1.20			2.12		
Ether	3.04	1.92	2.10	3.20	2.20	1.63		
Halothane	0.87	0.75	0.82	0.95	0.76	0.67	0.88	1.25
Isoflurane	1.50	1.15		1.38		1.31		
Methoxyflurane	0.23	0.16	0.23	0.22	0.13	0.22		
Nitrous oxide[b]	200	101	136			190		

[a]Data from Stimpfel and Gershey, 1991; Eger, 1978. Lower MAC values in % end-tidal concentrations indicate greater potency.

[b]MAC values for nitrous oxide are derived from hyperbaric studies to establish potency. Greater than 100% anesthetic is not possible in clinical situations.

Nitrous oxide is not commonly used as an anesthetic for laboratory animals and probably should not be, for two reasons. Its analgesic potency is low—the MAC (Table 5-2) exceeds 100% end-tidal concentration of the anesthetic for most species (Stimpfel and Gershey, 1991)—and it is potentially toxic to the reproductive system and bone marrow of personnel when used alone or in combination with other volatile agents without appropriate ventilation (Stoelting, 1987).

The end-tidal concentration of an inhalational agent is established by collecting a sample of gas from the endotracheal tube at the end of exhalation. Usually, a small needle is placed in the endotracheal tube and sealed to prevent leaks. Sampling should start when a state of equilibrium has been achieved at the concentration being delivered. With modern agents (e.g., halothane and isoflurane), that occurs after the induction of anesthesia when a predetermined level of anesthetic has been maintained for 10-15 minutes (Soma et al., 1988a). End-tidal samples can be collected in animals that weigh 1-2 kg with a 1-ml gastight syringe; small amounts of gas are collected at each breath until the volume of gas necessary for measurement has been collected. In larger animals, a greater volume can be collected at each breath; the volume of gas collected at each breath should be scaled to the size of the animal, to prevent dilution of the end-tidal sample with gas in the anesthetic equipment.

Gas samples collected with a syringe can be measured with a gas chromatograph calibrated for the specific anesthetic agent. Quadripole mass spectrometers also have been developed for respiratory-gas and anesthetic-gas measurements; their use allows breath-by-breath analysis of all exhaled gas (Marquette Gas Analysis Corp., St. Louis, Mo.; Brueland Kjaer Institute, Marlborough, Mass.). Gas-specific anesthetic monitors that allow breath-by-breath continuous monitoring of an inhalational agent are available (Puritan Bennett Corp., Kansas City, Mo.; Sensor Medics Corp., Anaheim, Calif.; Biochem International, Waukesha, Wis.). The continuous monitors might not be suitable for animals smaller than cats, because continuous flows of gas are necessary at 50 ml/min to measure end-tidal samples; in these circumstances, continuous flows will dilute the end-tidal sample and produce a concentration lower than the true one.

Intravenous Anesthesia

Inhalational anesthesia is often preferred for major surgical procedures, but steady-state anesthesia with some drugs can also can be obtained through intravenous administration. The ideal method to establish a steady-state level of anesthesia is to use pharmacokinetic measurements to calculate loading and infusion rates. The pharmacokinetic values used are the disposition and elimination rate constants of a drug in a particular species. Those vary with species, but they have been developed for many drugs in many species (Rigg et al., 1981; Pry-Roberts and Hug, 1984; Soma and Klide, 1987; Ludders, 1992).

BARBITURATES

Common Examples

Ultra-short-acting methylated oxybarbiturates (methohexital and hexobarbital) and thiobarbiturates (thiopental, thialbarbital, and thiamylal), short-acting oxybarbiturates (pentobarbital), and long-acting oxybarbiturates (phenobarbital).

Clinical Use

The barbiturates are widely used and versatile. They are classified as sedative-hypnotics on the basis of their use in humans to produce sedation. In veterinary anesthesia, they are used primarily to induce and maintain general anesthesia. An important distinction between the actions of the sedative-hypnotic barbiturates and the inhalational anesthetics and the actions of other drugs described in this chapter is that progressive increases in the dose of barbiturates and inhalational anesthetics produces progressive depression of the CNS and all physiologic functions, which leads to the loss of consciousness and even to death.

The barbiturates are classified according to their duration of action. The ultra-short-acting barbiturates are commonly used to induce anesthesia before maintenance with the inhalational anesthetics. The amount necessary is less than that required for surgical intervention; all that is necessary is anesthesia of adequate depth to produce sufficient muscle relaxation for tracheal intubation. A likely dose for this purpose is approximately 8-12 mg/kg. The final dose depends on the degree of sedation produced by drugs used for preanesthetic medication. Deep sedation produced by opioids requires lower induction doses of ultra-short-acting barbiturates than are required when no preanesthetic is used.

The ultra-short-acting thiopental, thialbarbital, and thiamylal are used principally to induce anesthesia; they are followed by maintenance with an inhalational agent or used alone for short periods.

The long-acting phenobarbital is used primarily in anticonvulsant therapy or for prolonged sedation.

Pharmacologic Effects

The short duration of the ultra-short-acting thiobarbiturates is the result of a rapid decrease in plasma and therefore brain concentration. The rapid decrease is due to rapid distribution into nonnervous tissue—initially into highly perfused visceral tissues (heart, brain, liver, spleen, etc.) and then into muscle and fat. The final elimination of the drug is through metabolism and renal excretion of metabolites. The ultra-short action of the methylated oxybarbiturate methohexital is attributed to rapid metabolism, rather than redistribution into nonnervous tissues. The short-acting barbiturate pentobarbital is biotransformed in the same way as methohexital, but at a lower rate. All clinically used barbiturates are metabolized by the liver, except phenobarbital, which is excreted intact by the kidneys.

The barbiturates belong to a group of agents that depress the CNS in a nonselective and dose-dependent manner (Gilman et al., 1990). Barbiturates depress respiratory drive by reducing CNS response to the stimulatory effects of CO_2; at high doses, the hypoxic respiratory drive is also suppressed. Barbiturates also depress protective reflexes, such as coughing and laryngeal reflexes. Under light anesthesia, the reflexes are present, and intubation of the trachea stimulates cough and laryngeal closure. Deep anesthesia abolishes those reflexes. Barbiturates, like other general anesthetics, reduce blood pressure, cardiac output, and renal blood flow, but increase or do not change heart rate. Barbiturates are poor analgesics and poor muscle relaxants compared with other general anesthetics, and they require deeper anesthesia for surgery. The effects and dosage of barbiturates are markedly affected by other CNS depressants, and the dose should be modified according to the administration of preanesthetic medication.

Dose Recommendations (Table 5-3)

The ultra-short-acting thiobarbiturates can be given rapidly intravenously. Their transfer from plasma to brain is very rapid, because of their high lipid solubility, and the effect of an injection is noted quickly. Later doses should be given slowly, carefully, and at short intervals to attain the desired depth of anesthesia.

The most commonly used short-acting barbiturate is sodium pentobarbital. The safest method of administration is the intravenous route. Oral, intraperitoneal, intramuscular, and even subcutaneous routes have been used, but they are less reliable for induction, are less consistent in recovery time, and can cause sloughing of tissue when injected perivascularly because of the high pH of their solutions (pH, 10 or above). Sodium pentobarbital is usually supplied as a 6% solution (60 mg/ml). If it is to be administered to smaller species, it should first be diluted (1:1 or 30 mg/ml for intravenous use, and 1:9 or 6 mg/ml for intraperitoneal use) to achieve a better control of the dose.

The recommended method of anesthetizing healthy animals with intravenous pentobarbital is to inject rapidly one-third to one-half the total calculated dose and then slowly infuse more to the desired depth of anesthesia. Ill animals are at an increased risk of effects of anesthesia and require less anesthetic. The oxybarbiturates (including pentobarbital) transfer across the blood-brain barrier slowly. Thus, an initial rapid injection is recommended to produce a high initial plasma concentration to avoid the excitement that can occur during the induction of anesthesia with pentobarbital.

Because veins are often not readily accessible in laboratory rodents, the most common route of administration of pentobarbital is intraperitoneal. Slower induction, longer recovery, more variable anesthesia, and a greater mortality rate can be

TABLE 5-3   Doses of Barbiturates in Various Species

Species	Drug	Dose, mg/kg (Route[a])	References
Dog and cat	Pentobarbital	25-30 (iv)	Warren, 1983
	Thiopental	8-30 (iv)	Warren, 1983
	Thiamylal	6-25 (iv)	Warren, 1983
Guinea pig	Pentobarbital	15-30 (iv)	Hughes et al., 1975
	Thiopental	20 (iv)	Hughes et al., 1975
Hamster	Pentobarbital	50-90 (ip)	Hughes, 1981
	Thiopental	20 (iv)	Vanderlip and Gilroy, 1981
Mouse	Pentobarbital	40-90 (ip)	Hughes, 1981; Clifford, 1984
	Thiopental	25-50 (iv)	Hughes, 1981; Clifford, 1984
	Thiamylal	25-50 (iv)	Harkness and Wagner, 1983; Clifford, 1984
Rabbit	Pentobarbital	40 (ip)	Vanderlip and Gilroy, 1981
	Pentobarbital	20-40 (iv)	Hughes, 1981
	Thiopental	15-50 (iv)	Sedgewick, 1980; Hughes, 1981
	Thiamylal	15-30 (iv)	Sedgewick, 1980; Vanderlip and Gilroy, 1981
Rat	Pentobarbital	25-45 (ip)	Hughes, 1981; Clifford, 1984
	Thiopental	20-25 (iv)	Sedgewick, 1980; Clifford, 1984
	Thiamylal	20-50 (iv)	Sedgewick, 1980; Clifford, 1984

[a]iv = intravenous; ip = intraperitoneal.

expected with intraperitoneal administration. Excitement can occur during the induction period because of the slow absorption from the peritoneal cavity.

Variability in dose and sleeping time has been reported, especially in rats and mice. A dose range of 30-60 mg/kg has been reported for rodents (Wixson et al., 1987a), but doses as high as 90 mg/kg have also been given (Hughes, 1981). The short-acting pentobarbital can be used in smaller species of laboratory and companion animals for 2-3 hours of general anesthesia.

Sex, age, diet, type of bedding, and strain have been suggested as reasons for dose variability (Harkness and Wagner, 1983; Clifford, 1984). Therefore, a specific dose might have to be established for a given colony of rodents. Variability has also been noted in rabbits.

DISSOCIATIVE ANESTHETICS—CYCLOHEXAMINES

Common Example

Ketamine hydrochloride and tiletamine-zolazepam combination (Telazol®).

Clinical Use

Ketamine is the cyclohexamine most commonly used for sedation, analgesia, and anesthesia. The cyclohexamines have been categorized as sympathomimetic anesthetics that produce a state of anesthesia termed "dissociative." The original preparation, phencyclidine hydrochloride (Sernylan®), was used in cats, nonhuman primates, and some wild species, but had a prolonged recovery. It has been withdrawn from the market because of its potential for human abuse. The cyclohexamines have analgesic properties in low doses and produce a state of general anesthesia at higher doses. The analgesic and anesthetic properties of ketamine in most rodents are poor, and it does not produce surgical anesthesia when used alone in the rat (Wilson and Wheatley, 1981), except in very high doses that produce severe respiratory depression (Lumb and Jones, 1984; Flecknell, 1987). Many investigators believe that it should be administered in combination with a sedative, such as diazepam or xylazine (Flecknell, 1987). Ketamine has been used successfully as a preanesthetic agent before the use of inhalational agents in rodents and rabbits (Wass et al., 1974; White et al., 1975).

It is desirable to administer atropine before ketamine in some species to minimize the excessive salivary and bronchial secretions associated with ketamine. Xylazine and diazepam are excellent adjuncts to the use of ketamine to produce surgical anesthesia in cats, dogs, guinea pigs, hamsters, horses, rabbits, sheep, pigs, and primates (Tables 5-4 and 5-5). The combination of xylazine or diazepam with ketamine permits smoother induction of anesthesia and deeper and longer-lasting anesthesia than ketamine alone (Wixson et al., 1987a,b,c).

Pharmacologic Effects

Ketamine anesthesia is not accompanied by the classic, progressive CNS depression that is noted after use of barbiturates and inhalational agents; rather, it is a cataleptic anesthetic state (Winters et al., 1972; Chen, 1973). In many species, it produces an appearance similar to that of decerebration, including hypertonicity of the antigravity muscles and an apneustic respiratory pattern that is characterized by breathholding at the peak of inspiration followed by passive exhalation (Calderwood et al., 1971).

The characteristic clinical signs seen in animals after the administration of ketamine are head weaving, progressive ataxia, complete loss of coordination, collapse, and immobilization. There are usually increases in muscle tone, salivation, and bronchial secretions; muscle twitching; and, while the animal is under anesthesia, spontaneous movements unrelated to surgical stimuli. Ocular, oral, and swallowing reflexes are present, and the animal's eyes remain open with corneal and pupillary reflexes present. Nystagmus might occur, and lacrimal secretions persist. An increase in respiration might occur, but death from the high dose necessary for surgical anesthesia is eventually due to respiratory depression (Flecknell, 1987), especially in small rodents. Ketamine has been used for general anesthesia in humans; studies have shown dose-related analgesic and anesthetic properties (Sadove et al., 1971).

Cats exhibit an apneustic respiratory pattern and extensor rigidity of the limbs. The rigidity remains during the peak effect of the drug and gradually subsides during recovery. The tremors and muscle rigidity are not as prevalent in nonhuman primates as they are in other animals. Lacrimal secretions persist, and atropine is recommended to reduce salivation.

Dose Recommendations (Tables 5-4 and 5-5)

Generally, the effect lasts less than an hour in most species. If anesthesia lasting longer than an hour is desirable, inhalational anesthetics might be a better choice.

Ketamine is useful alone for restraining cats and can be administered to healthy animals subcutaneously, intramuscularly, or intravenously over a dose range of 2-33 mg/kg (Wright, 1982; Muir et al., 1989). It is the drug of choice for restraining primates (Flecknell, 1987). Intramuscular doses of ketamine alone or with adjuncts for several primate species are shown in Table 5-4.

Telazol®, a combination of tiletamine hydrochloride and zolazepam, is approved for use in dogs and cats. The two drugs are combined in a 1:1 ratio, and

TABLE 5-4   Dose Ranges of Ketamine Administered Intramuscularly in Primates

Species	Dose, mg/kg	Adjunct Drug, mg/kg	Comments	References
Baboon	10	Diazepam, 7.5	Light anesthesia	Woofson et al., 1980
Chimpanzee	7-10	None	Light anesthesia	Bonner et al., 1972
Gorilla (lowland)	8-10	None	Light anesthesia	Bonner et al., 1972
Rhesus	7	Xylazine	Anesthesia (not recommended)	Reutlinger et al., 1980
Rhesus	11	Acepromazine, 0.55	Light anesthesia	Connoly and Quimby, 1978
Orangutan	9-12	None	Light anesthesia	Bonner et al., 1972
Patus (red)	6-12	None	Restraint	Sanford and Meacham, 1978
Pigtail	2	None	Anesthesia	Hargrove et al., 1980
Squirrel	13	None	Restraint	Greenstein, 1975
Squirrel	25	None	Anesthesia	Greenstein, 1975

TABLE 5-5 Doses of Ketamine[a] and Adjunct Drugs in Nonprimate Species

Species	Dose, mg/kg (Route[b])	Adjunct Drug, mg/kg (Route[b])	Comments	References
Cat	4.4-6.6 (iv)	Diazepam, 0.44 (iv)	Anesthesia	Muir et al., 1989
	10-22 (im, sc)	Xylazine, 1.1 (im)	Anesthesia (20-30 min)	Cullen and Jones, 1977; Flecknell, 1987
	2.2-6.6 (iv)	Xylazine, 0.66 (iv)	Anesthesia	Muir et al., 1989
Calf	4.4-10 (im)	Xylazine, 0.1 (im)	Anesthesia (30-40 min)	Trim, 1987
Chinchilla	40 (im)	Xylazine, 0.5 (im)	Anesthesia (40-60 min)	Morgan et al., 1981
Dog	4.4-6.6 (iv)	Xylazine, 0.33 (iv)	Anesthesia	Muir et al., 1989
	6.6 (iv)	Xylazine, 0.66 (iv)	Anesthesia	Muir et al., 1989
	11 (iv)	Xylazine, 1.1 (iv)	Anesthesia	Kolata and Rawlings, 1982
Guinea pig	44 (im)	Acetylpromazine, 2.0 (im)	Anesthesia (1.5 h)	Shucard et al., 1975
	60 (im)	Xylazine, 8 (im)	Sedation, relaxation	Green et al., 1981b
	40 (ip)	Xylazine, 5 (ip)	Light anesthesia	Flecknell, 1987; Harvey and Walberg, 1987
Hamster	200 (ip)	Xylazine, 10 (ip)	Anesthesia	Curl and Peters, 1983
Hamster	80 (ip)	Xylazine, 16 (ip)	Sedation, relaxation	Green et al., 1981b
Horse	2.2 (iv)	Xylazine, 1.1 (iv)	Light anesthesia	Kaka et al., 1979; Short, 1987; Muir et al., 1989

Rabbit	30 (im)	Diazepam, 5.0 (im)	Sedation, relaxation	Green et al., 1981b
	30 (im)	Xylazine, 2.0 (im)	Sedation, relaxation	Green et al., 1981b
	10 (iv)	Xylazine, 3.0 (iv)	Anesthesia (30 min)	Flecknell, 1987
	35 (im)	Xylazine, 5.0 (im)	Anesthesia (45-60 min)	Sanford and Colby, 1980
	50 (im)	Paraldehyde, 0.5 (im)	Anesthesia (2-4 h)	Kisloff, 1975
Rat	10 (ip)	Xylazine, 3.0 (ip)	Anesthesia (30 min)	Flecknell, 1987
Rat	80 (ip)	Xylazine, 12 (ip)	Sedation, relaxation	Green et al., 1981b
Sheep	22-44 (im, iv)	Acetylpromazine, 0.55 (iv)	Anesthesia (1-1.5 h)	Thurmon et al., 1973
Sheep and	10 (im)	Xylazine, 0.1 (im)	Anesthesia (30-40 min)	Trim, 1987
	10 (im)	Diazepam, 0.2-0.5 (im)	Anesthesia (30-40 min)	Trim, 1987
Swine	2 (iv)	Xylazine 2.0 (iv) plus oxymorphone, 0.75 (iv)	Anesthesia (20-30 min), double each dose for im	Breese and Dodman, 1984
Swine	10 (iv, im)	Xylazine, 1.0 (iv, im)	Anesthesia (10 min)	Trim and Gilroy, 1985

[a]Tiletamine, similar in pharmacologic properties to ketamine, is combined with zolazepam in the proprietary preparation Telazol. Actions and dose of Telazol are discussed in the text.

[b]iv = intravenous; im = intramuscular; sc = subcutaneous; ip = intraperitoneal.

the dose is expressed as a combined total dose. Tiletamine, a congener of phencyclidine, is similar in its pharmacologic properties to ketamine (it produces, e.g., catalepsy, seizures, and clonic and tonic muscle contractions), but it is 2-3 times as potent. The benzodiazepine zolazepam, when combined with tiletamine, potentiates its anesthetic effect with improved muscle relaxation, absence of tremors, and a smoother recovery. Telazol is used for many diagnostic and surgical procedures in dogs, cats, and wild animals (Short, 1987; Muir et al., 1989). In cats, it has been used for surgical procedures, including abdominal surgery, over a dose range of 6-16 mg/kg; anesthesia persisted for 32-135 minutes (Ward et al., 1974). Cardiorespiratory effects over a dose range of 10-24 mg/kg included transient reductions in blood pressure and aortic blood flow and apnea at higher doses (Hellyer et al., 1988). In calves, Telazol produced rapid induction, good to excellent muscle relaxation, minimal regurgitation or bloat, and minimal cardiovascular changes over a dose range of 4-12 mg/kg (Lin et al., 1989). The duration of effect was approximately an hour. Similar effects were reported for sheep (Ward et al., 1974). Although Telazol was found to be unsatisfactory for use in rabbits and guinea pigs, it did produce a dose-related sleeping time at 20-30 mg/kg of 41-110 minutes (Ward et al., 1974). In some species, multiple doses of Telazol are associated with prolonged recovery characterized by bizarre behavior.

NEUROLEPTANALGESICS

Common Example

Innovar-Vet®.

Clinical Use

Neuroleptanalgesia, which is produced by the combination of an opioid and a tranquilizer, is defined as a state of CNS depression and analgesia without unconsciousness. States of deep sedation and analgesia adequate for surgery have been induced in dogs, nonhuman primates, and humans (Nilsson and Janssen, 1961; Marsboom et al., 1962, 1963; Soma and Shields, 1964; Field et al., 1966). Neuroleptanalgesia is demonstrated by people's ability to acknowledge verbal commands and dogs' and rats' ability to respond to auditory stimuli, despite analgesia and CNS depression (Jones and Simmons, 1968). A sharp noise, such as that made by the dropping of an object or the crumpling of paper, will evoke a response. Movement might be slight and consists of lifting of the head and some limb movement. That response persists, despite the reduction in or complete absence of a pedal reflex.

Neuroleptanalgesia is useful for minor surgical procedures in combination with regional anesthesia in dogs, and it has been used for abdominal surgery in rodents. It can substitute for a general anesthetic for many diagnostic procedures, and at lower doses it is excellent for restraint. Neuroleptanalgesia can be used in conjunction with local anesthesia for some surgical procedures, including laparotomy and enucleation, and with restraint for such procedures as orbital bleeding in laboratory rodents.

Pharmacologic Effects

Innovar-Vet has been used extensively in veterinary medicine. It contains the potent opioid fentanyl at 0.4 mg/ml and the tranquilizer droperidol at 20 mg/ml. Other tranquilizers and opioids can also be used in combination to produce a similar effect (Green, 1975; Green et al., 1981a). The combination of fentanyl and droperidol is only one suggested combination.

Major actions of the combination are primarily those of the opioid. Panting can occur in dogs, but the overall effect on respiration is depression, and all animals should be watched carefully when high doses are administered. Fentanyl can produce marked bradycardia, which can be prevented by the prior administration of atropine or reversed by intravenous administration of atropine. Droperidol can induce vasodilation and hypotension because of its α_2-adrenergic blocking activity.

Dose Recommendations (Table 5-6)

Innovar-Vet is commonly administered intramuscularly, but can be administered intravenously and subcutaneously. The broad dose range among species reflects not only species variation, but the wide margin of safety of neuroleptanalgesia. Doses at the lower end of a range are intended for minor procedures; doses at the upper end should be used for surgery.

In dogs, maximal analgesia is sustained for 30-40 minutes with a single effective dose. Beyond that period, a reaction to a noxious cutaneous stimulus might occur, although generalized sedation and some analgesia are still evident. Emergence delirium does not occur. Within 60-90 minutes after intramuscular injection of Innovar-Vet, most dogs can maintain sternal recumbency and respond to auditory stimuli by lifting their heads and looking around. Some dogs attempt to stand. Most will regain their righting and ambulatory capabilities within 2 hours of injection.

OPIOID AGONISTS, AGONIST-ANTAGONISTS, AND ANTAGONISTS

Common Examples

Opioid agonists (morphine, meperidine, oxymorphone, and fentanyl), opioid antagonists (naloxone), and opioid agonist-antagonists (pentazocine, butorphanol, nalbuphine, and buprenorphine).

TABLE 5-6   Doses of Innovar-Vet® in Laboratory Animals

Species	Dose, ml/kg (Route[a])	Reference
Anthropoids and lower monkeys	0.1-0.2	Marsboom et al., 1963
Baboon, mangabey, pigtail	0.03-2.2	Field et al., 1966
Cat	0.10	Muir et al., 1989
Dog	0.01-0.02 0.03-0.7 (iv)	Soma and Shields, 1964 Muir et al., 1989
Guinea pig	0.08-0.66 0.44-0.88 0.16	Hughes, 1981 Rubright and Thayer, 1970, 1971; Leash et al., 1973 Jones and Simmons, 1968; Walden, 1978
Mouse	2 5 0.01	Hughes et al., 1975 Lewis and Jennings, 1972 Jones and Simmons, 1968; Walden, 1978
Pig	0.05 (iv) (<90 kg) 0.025 (iv) (>90 kg)	Muir et al., 1989 Muir et al., 1989
Rabbit	0.15-0.17 0.22 0.30	Vanderlip and Gilroy, 1981 Strack and Kaplan, 1968 Walden, 1978
Rat	0.1-0.3 0.40 0.26	Hughes, 1981 Wixson et al., 1987a,b,c Jones and Simmons, 1968

[a]Intramuscularly administered unless otherwise indicated.
iv = intravenous.

Clinical Use

The sedation and analgesia produced by the agonists are important in veterinary medicine for restraining fearful and anxious animals and most especially for controlling pain. Intravenous agonists can be used for general anesthesia when combined with other drugs. When used properly, intravenous agonists are cardio-vascular-sparing and produce the least cardiovascular depression of all the anesthetic techniques.

Agonists can be used in dogs, nonhuman primates, and, in some cases, horses and cats to control pain. Because agonists can excite sheep, goats, pigs, rats, mice, lagomorphs, and guinea pigs, they are not administered alone, but they can be combined with other sedatives and tranquilizers and used for sedation, restraint, and analgesia for minor surgical procedures.

Agonist-antagonists are designed to stimulate selectively the opioid receptors that produce desirable effects, such as analgesia and mild sedation, while blocking the receptors that produce undesirable effects of cardiac and respiratory depression. Agonist-antagonists can partially reverse the analgesic, cardiovascular, and respiratory depressant effects of opioid agonists, such as the opioid component of neuroleptanalgesics (Flecknell et al., 1989).

The antagonist naloxone hydrochloride is used to reverse the sedative and depressant effects of the opioids when they have been used for temporary restraint for diagnostic procedures, transport, or minor surgery or when an overdose has been administered. The antagonists are also useful when neuroleptanalgesics are used; when effects of the opioid component is reversed, the animal will be alert and ambulatory. The effects of the tranquilizer component are not reversed by naloxone, and some sedation remains evident. Naloxone used alone does not produce any observable depressant, respiratory, or cardiovascular effects.

The available agonist-antagonist drugs act as agonists at some opioid receptors and as antagonists at other opioid receptors, thus providing a complex pharmacology. They are used as analgesics, but might have less respiratory depressant and sedative action than the opioid agonists.

Pharmacologic Effects

The term *opioid* is used generically as a designation for all endogenous and exogenous substances that bind to a subset of opioid receptors (Gilman et al., 1990). They are typified by morphine and have morphine-like actions. Not all the drugs in this class might have the total pharmacologic profile and actions of morphine (Martin, 1984), but they are all displaced from the opioid receptors by the antagonist naloxone. Antagonists bind to the same receptors as morphine and other opioid analgesics, but have little or no analgesic or other agonist action themselves. They displace agents like morphine from the receptors and so are used to reverse the actions of agonists.

The agonist-antagonists are compounds that have been synthesized as part of the effort to develop effective analgesics with minimal abuse potential. They are similar to morphine, in that they attach to opioid receptors, but are more receptor-specific in their use as analgesics. They also have both agonist and antagonist actions at opioid receptors.

All three of these classes of drugs act to produce their effects at four receptors: mu, delta, kappa, and sigma receptors. Actions at mu receptors produce sedation, analgesia, and respiratory depression and probably contribute to physical dependence in people and in animals. Actions at delta receptors might produce analgesia at the level of the spinal cord, but probably have more prominent, nonanalgesic effects supraspinally (e.g., convulsions). Actions at kappa receptors produce analgesia, particularly at the level of the spinal cord, and actions at sigma receptors produce dysphoria and hallucinations. Agonists, like morphine, appear to stimulate all opioid receptors, producing a variety of desirable effects (e.g., analgesia) and undesirable effects (e.g., respiratory depression). Antagonists, like naloxone, have high affinity for all opioid receptors and thus displace and block the effects of opioid agonists.

Depending on the species, the effects of opioids in animals can be excitement and sedation. Excitement is characterized by mydriasis, nausea, panting, increased heart rate, sweating, pacing, head pressing, increased spinal-reflex activity, and convulsions. Specific clinical signs are species-related and drug- and dose-dependent. The sedative effects of the opioids are miosis, respiratory depression, bradycardia, hypothermia, and reductions in reflex activity and response to external stimuli. The effects in dogs are biphasic and dose-related: depression and analgesia at the lower, therapeutic doses and almost strychnine-like convulsions and death at the higher doses (Reynolds and Randall, 1957). Sedation is achieved at the expense of respiratory and cardiovascular compromise, especially when other drugs are added to produce general anesthesia or deep sedation.

That the administration of morphine and other opioids to postsurgical or recumbent dogs and cats by intramuscular injection or slow intravenous infusion rarely produces emesis suggests that involvement of the vestibular system contributes to opioid-induced emesis (Stoelting, 1987). However, emesis often occurs when opioids are given as preanesthetics.

Dose Recommendations (Table 5-7)

The dose administered can vary with the clinical objective, i.e., preanesthetic use, sedation, or analgesic control of pain. If an opioid is given in conjunction with other CNS-depressant drugs, it might be desirable to reduce the dose of opioid.

Agonists: A sedative dose of morphine for a dog (0.5 mg/kg) will produce restlessness in a cat. At lower doses (0.1 mg/kg) administered during recovery from anesthesia, morphine was found to be beneficial in cats (Heavner, 1970). Higher doses can be administered to cats if tranquilizers, such as promazine or acepromazine, or other depressants are administered simultaneously, thereby depressing the excitatory effects of opioids. When agonists are used as preanesthetic sedatives, general anesthetic agents should be administered carefully and in reduced amounts, to prevent respiratory depression. Use of morphine and other opioids alone in farm animals (cow, sheep, goat, and pig) is not recommended, because they produce excitement. Morphine combined with xylazine can be used for analgesia and restraint in horses (Klein and Baetjer, 1974).

Nonhuman primates and dogs respond to morphine in a dual manner, lower doses producing sedation and larger doses convulsions. For sedation adequate to enable safe management of most nonhuman primates, the doses suggested for dogs,

TABLE 5-7   Doses of Opioid Agonists and Opioid Agonist-Antagonists in Various Species[a]

Species	Drug	Dose, mg/kg (Route[b])	Reference
Cat	Oxymorphone	0.2 (iv, im)	Harvey and Walberg, 1987
	Oxymorphone	0.2 (sc)	Short, 1987
	Morphine	0.05-0.1 (iv)	Harvey and Walberg, 1987
	Pentazocine	1.5-3.0 (im, sc)	Harvey and Walberg, 1987
	Butorphanol	0.1-0.8 (iv, im)	Sawyer and Rech, 1987
	Meperidine	5-10 (iv)	Sawyer and Rech, 1987
	Nalbuphine	0.75-3.0 (iv, im, sc)	Flecknell, 1987; Sawyer and Rech, 1987
Dog	Morphine	0.5-1.0 (im, sc)	Harvey and Walberg, 1987
	Oxymorphone	0.2-0.4 (iv, im)	Harvey and Walberg, 1987
	Meperidine	2-6 (sc)	Copland et al., 1987
	Fentanyl	0.04 (im, sc)	Harvey and Walberg, 1987
	Pentazocine	1.5-3.0 (iv, im)	Harvey and Walberg, 1987
	Butorphanol	0.2-0.8 (im, sc)	Sawyer et al., 1991
Guinea pig	Morphine	10 (im, sc)	Wright et al., 1985
	Meperidine	1-2 (im, sc)	Hughes, 1981
	Pentazocine	1-3 (im)	Vanderlip and Gilroy, 1981; Hughes, 1981
Horse	Meperidine	2.2 (im)	Lowe, 1969
	Butorphanol	0.1-0.4 (iv)	Kalpravidh et al., 1984
	Butorphanol	0.01-0.04 (iv)	Orsini, 1988; Kohn and Muir, 1988
Mouse	Morphine	10-20 (sc)	Flecknell, 1984
	Morphine	2-5 (ip)	Clifford, 1984
	Meperidine	20-60 (im, sc)	Hughes, 1981
	Pentazocine	10 (sc)	Harvey and Walberg, 1987
	Pentazocine	2-3 (im)	Vanderlip and Gilroy, 1981
	Butorphanol	5.4 (sc)	Harvey and Walberg, 1987
Primate	Morphine	1-2 (im, sc)	Flecknell, 1987
	Meperidine	2-4 (im)	Harvey and Walberg, 1987
	Fentanyl	0.05-0.1 (iv, im)	Field et al., 1966
	Pentazocine	2-5 (sc)	Harvey and Walberg, 1987
Rabbit	Morphine	5 (im, ip)	Flecknell, 1984
	Meperidine	10 (sc)	Hughes, 1981; Flecknell, 1984
	Pentazocine	10-20 (im, sc)	Flecknell, 1984
Rat	Morphine	10 (im, sc)	Flecknell, 1984
	Meperidine	25-50 (im, sc)	Clifford, 1984; Hughes, 1981
	Pentazocine	10 (sc)	Wright et al., 1985
	Pentazocine	2-3 (im)	Vanderlip and Gilroy, 1981
	Butorphanol	23.3 (sc)	Harvey and Walberg, 1987

[a]See Table 5-8 for buphrenorphine.

[b]iv = intraveneous; im = intramuscular; sc = subcutaneous; ip = intraperitoneal.

or slightly higher doses, are necessary. Good agreement was found in the transposition of relative drug potencies from monkeys to humans (Malis, 1973).

Meperidine can be combined with a tranquilizer to produce sedation in cats and other animals in which excitement can occur (Clifford, 1957). The dose of meperidine in nonrodents, with or without a tranquilizer, should not exceed 10 mg/kg by the intramuscular route. The lack of marked sedation after the use of meperidine or other opioids in cats and other animals that lack the classic response to opioids should not mislead clinicians into administering general anesthetics and other depressants later at normal rates and dosages.

Meperidine also has been used in rats, rabbits, guinea pigs, and mice (Hughes, 1981). The doses in rodents are variable and generally higher than in nonrodents. The durations of analgesic action of meperidine in rats at 5, 10, and 20 mg/kg were 2, 45, and 72 minutes, respectively. At the time of disappearance of analgesia, the plasma concentrations were similar (200-220 ng/ml) after the three different doses (Dahlstrom et al., 1979).

In horses and ponies, meperidine has been used for pain, especially after gastrointestinal and orthopedic surgery. The suggested dose is 2.2 mg/kg administered intramuscularly; it should not be given intravenously.

The analgesic effect of oxymorphone in dogs and cats has long been recognized (Palminteri, 1963). Oxymorphone has been shown to have several important advantages over morphine and meperidine in dogs (Copland et al., 1987). For example, it does not promote histamine release and associated vasodilation and bronchoconstriction; as a preanesthetic, it is less likely than morphine to provoke emesis.

A study is under way to develop a canine pain scaling approach to assess several postsurgical canine behaviors with and without the administration of oxymorphone (Hansen et al., 1990). Behaviors are being correlated with plasma concentrations of stress hormones, physiologic signs, type of surgery, and amount of tissue trauma. The goal is to identify behaviors most likely associated with pain and stress, so that an objective basis can be established for diagnosing pain and optimizing analgesic therapy.

Agonist-antagonists: Analgesic and behavioral effects of butorphanol (0.1–0.8 mg/kv intravenously and subcutaneously) and nalbuphine and pentazocine (each at 0.75–3 mg/kg intravenously) have been compared in cats (Sawyer and Rech, 1987). Visceral analgesia was produced by all drugs over dose ranges given. However, somatic analgesia could be achieved with butorphanol at 0.8 mg/kg intravenously. Neither sedation nor behavioral effects were observed with any of the drugs over the dose ranges stated, except with higher doses of pentazocine. Sawyer and Rech (1987) recommended doses of butorphanol of 0.1–0.2 mg/kg intravenously or 0.4 mg/kg subcutaneously. In dogs, dose-dependent sedation occurred over a dose range of 0.1–0.4 mg/kg intravenously (Trim, 1983).

Buprenorphine, approved for use in the United States in 1989, has been recommended as an analgesic to alleviate moderate to severe pain in several laboratory animal species (Flecknell, 1987). Table 5-8 lists doses and recom-

TABLE 5-8   Doses of Buprenorphine in Various Species for Management of Moderate to Severe Pain

Species	Dose, mg/kg (Route[a])	Dose Interval, hours	Reference
Cat	0.005-0.01 (iv, sc)	12	Clifford, 1957; Flecknell, 1987
Dog	0.01-0.02 (im, sc) 0.01-0.02 (iv, im, sc)	8-12 12	Harvey and Walberg, 1987; Flecknell, 1987
Guinea pig	0.05 (sc)	8-12	Flecknell, 1987
Mouse	2.5 (ip) 2.0 (sc)	6-8 12	Harvey and Walberg, 1987; Flecknell, 1987
Pig	0.1 (im)	12	Flecknell, 1987
Primate	0.01 (iv, im) 0.01 (iv, im)	8-12 12	Harvey and Walberg, 1987; Flecknell, 1987
Rabbit	0.02-0.05 (iv, sc)	8-12	Harvey and Walberg, 1987; Flecknell, 1987
Rat	0.02-0.08 (sc, ip) 0.1-0.5 (iv, sc)	8-12 8-12	Harvey and Walberg, 1987; Flecknell, 1987
Sheep and goat	0.005 (im)	4-6	Flecknell, 1987

[a]im = intramuscular; iv = intravenous; ip = intraperitoneal; sc = subcutaneous.

mended dose intervals to maintain the analgesic effect in several species. The actual dose interval used in an animal should depend on the analgesic needs of the animal.

Intrathecal and epidural administration of opioids and local anesthetics for postoperative analgesia (Gregg, 1989) and for intractable sacral and perineal pain (Finley, 1990) is gaining widespread use in human medicine. In dogs, the epidural administration of morphine has successfully provided prolonged postsurgical analgesia (Valverde et al., 1989). Its major advantage is the long duration of analgesia (10-23 hours) after an epidural dose of 0.1 mg/kg of body weight. (See also Dodman et al., 1992.)

Antagonists: Naloxone (0.04 mg/kg intravenously) is as effective in animals as in humans in reversing the analgesic, sedative, cardiovascular, and respiratory effect of opioid agonists.

NONSTEROIDAL ANTI-INFLAMMATORY DRUGS

Common Examples

Salicylates (aspirin), pyrazolones (phenylbutazone [Butazolidin®], oxyphenbutazone and dipyrone), anthranilic acids (mefenamic acid and meclofenamic acid), nicotinic acid derivatives (flunixin [Banamine®]), phenylpropionic acids (ibuprofen [Motrin®] and fenoprofen [Nalfon®]), naphthylpropionic acids (naproxen [Naprosyn®]), indoles (indomethacin [Indocin®]), and *p*-aminophenols (acetaminophen [Tylenol®]).

Clinical Use

The nonsteroidal anti-inflammatory drugs (NSAIDs) are commonly used in the treatment of myositis, arthritis, and other surgical and nonsurgical acute and chronic inflammatory conditions (Table 5-9). The NSAIDs are the preferred drugs for the treatment of acute and chronic inflammatory conditions, because they do not interfere with the secretion of glucocorticoids from the adrenal gland, as do the steroid drugs.

Pharmacologic Effects

The analgesic, antipyretic, and anti-inflammatory actions of NSAIDs are attributable mainly to inhibition of prostaglandin synthesis in the peripheral nervous system and CNS (e.g., antipyresis by inhibition of prostaglandin synthesis in the thermoregulatory center). Acetaminophen, however, is considered to have poor anti-inflammatory activity, because it is a weak prostaglandin synthetase inhibitor in vitro. The pain produced by the inflammatory process is mediated through endogenous eicosanoids and other substances (see Chapter 2). Many of the products of eicosanoid metabolism are responsible for the classic signs of the inflammatory process: redness, pain, and edema. Eicosanoids, released as a consequence of injury, produce vasodilation, increase in capillary permeability, edema, and leukocyte migration, which are associated with the pain produced by inflammation. The eicosanoids are not stored in cells, and their synthesis is initiated by the enzymatic release of fatty acids from cellular phospholipids (Higgins, 1985; Moore, 1985). The release of arachidonic acid from membrane phospholipids is the first event in the synthesis of the eicosanoids. Cyclo-oxygenase catalyzes the initial formation of prostaglandin from arachidonic acid. NSAIDs, with the possible exception of acetaminophen, are potent inhibitors of cyclo-oxygenase (Gilman et al., 1990).

The eicosanoids are synthesized by all cells except red blood cells and have a major effect on cellular functions. For example, the release of the eicosanoids or their blockage has an effect on the microcirculation, producing vasodilation or vasoconstriction. NSAIDs interfere with or modify the effects of many drugs that depend on the release of eicosanoids.

The postoperative use of NSAIDs to minimize inflammation associated with surgical trauma is encouraged. But they have a broad effect on the arachidonic acid cascade, so they can modify the actions of many drugs and normal physiologic activity that might be under study. Because they do not produce obvious behavioral changes, as do many other drugs used for the relief of pain and distress, these

TABLE 5-9 Doses of Nonsteroidal Anti-inflammatory Drugs

Species	Drug	Dose, mg/kg (Route[a])	Dose Interval, hours	References
Cat	Aspirin	10 (po)	48	Jenkins, 1987
Dog	Aspirin	10 (po)	6-8	Booth and McDonald, 1982
	Ibuprofen	10 (po)	24-48	Jenkins, 1987
	Flunixin	1.1 (iv, im)		Hardie et al., 1985
	Acetaminophen	15 (po)	8	Jenkins, 1987
	Phenylbutazone	15 (po)	8	Booth and McDonald, 1982
Horse	Aspirin	25 (po)	12	Jenkins, 1987
	Flunixin	1.1 (iv, im, po)		Houdeshell and Hennessey, 1977; Soma et al., 1988b
	Phenylbutazone	4.4 (iv, po)	12-24	Piperno et al., 1968
Mice	Aspirin	120-300 (po)		Jenkins, 1987
	Ibuprofen	7.5 (po)		Jenkins, 1987
	Acetaminophen	300 (ip)		Jenkins, 1987
Primate	Aspirin	20 (po)	6-8	Flecknell, 1987
Rabbit	Aspirin	500 (po)		CCAC, 1980
Rat	Aspirin	100 (po)	4	Flecknell, 1987
	Ibuprofen	10-30 (po)		Jenkins, 1987
	Acetaminophen	110-300 (po)		Jenkins, 1987
	Phenylbutazone	30-100 (po)		Kruckenberg, 1979
	Phenylbutazone	7.5-15 (sc)		Kruckenberg, 1979
Ruminant	Aspirin	50-100 (po)	12	Jenkins, 1987
	Phenylbutazone	6 (iv, im, po)		Eberhardson et al., 1979

[a]iv = intravenous; im = intramuscular; ip = intraperitoneal; sc = subcutaneous; po = oral.

interactions might not be considered. Drugs other than NSAIDs (for example, corticosteroids) can also modify the release of arachidonic acid and can interfere with experimental studies.

NSAIDs share many properties; all are effective analgesics, antipyretics, and (except for acetaminophen) potent anti-inflammatory agents. They also share the tendency to produce adverse effects on the gastrointestinal, renal, and, to a lesser extent, hepatic and hematopoietic systems. The tendency to induce toxic manifestations differs markedly among species and NSAIDs. Most NSAIDs are weak acids, are highly bound to serum proteins, and are biotransformed extensively by hepatic mixed-function oxidases. Differences in rates of drug biotransformation might underlie much of the variation among species in the elimination kinetics of NSAIDs (Mazue et al., 1982)—for example, variation in the plasma half-life of aspirin (horse, 1 hour; dog, 8 hours; cat, 38 hours) and phenylbutazone (horse, 3-6 hours; cattle, 35-72 hours) (Jenkins, 1987). Such differences should be taken into account in the establishment of dose schedules to provide effective drug concentrations in the body during therapy and to prevent drug toxicity.

Dose Recommendations (Table 5-9)

Before NSAIDs are used, references should be consulted for more information on length of treatment and reactions specific to the animals in question. For example, acetaminophen should not be used in cats, because of deficiencies in detoxifying mechanisms and an inherent sensitivity of feline red blood cells to oxidative damage.

NSAIDS constitute a potentially valuable group of drugs for producing analgesia in laboratory animals. Dose recommendations are available for treating individual animals of a given species, but information on administration in drinking water (e.g., dose, stability, and palatability) is lacking and would be especially valuable for treating large numbers of animals, such as rodents, simultaneously with a minimum of handling.

SPECIAL ANESTHETIC CONSIDERATIONS

α-Chloralose

α-Chloralose (40-80 mg/kg intravenously) is useful for providing prolonged anesthesia for nonsurvival experiments (6-10 hours) with minimal cardiovascular and respiratory depression (Van Citters et al., 1964). However, the depth of analgesia is usually inadequate for surgical procedures (Flecknell, 1987; Holzgrefe et al., 1987), and its use for this purpose requires clear justification. When combined with adjunctive drugs in nonsurvival procedures, chloralose can be used for preparative surgery and later for maintenance (Holzgrefe et al., 1987). Its onset of action is slow (15 minutes after intravenous administration), so a short-acting barbiturate usually is given first to induce anesthesia. But chloralose can be administered to animals already deeply sedated with opioids, tranquilizers, or cyclohexamines.

Urethane

Urethane, like chloralose, produces prolonged anesthesia with minimal cardiovascular and respiratory depression. Unlike chloralose, it produces analgesia sufficient for surgical procedures. Urethane has been reported to be both mutagenic and carcinogenic, so it should be handled as a mild carcinogen, and animals anesthetized with it should not be allowed to recover (Flecknell, 1987).

Use of Skeletal Muscle Relaxants

Muscle relaxants do not provide relief from pain. They are used to paralyze skeletal muscles *while an animal is fully anesthetized.* If a procedure will cause no pain and the animal is properly ventilated, general anesthesia may be discontinued under carefully controlled conditions for specific neurophysiologic studies (Van Sluyters and Oberdorfer, 1991). Such use of muscle relaxants requires prior approval of an animal care and use committee, because acute stress is believed to be a consequence of paralysis in a conscious state. Table 5-10 lists doses of the neuromuscular blocking agent pancuronium, which is commonly used in experimental animals. Klein (1987) has compiled an extensive review of neuromuscular blocking agents and their use in dogs, cats, pigs, horses, sheep, and calves. This

TABLE 5-10   Doses of Pancuronium in Domestic Species

Species	Dose, mg/kg	Duration, minutes	Anesthetic	Reference
Calf	43 ± 9[a]	43 ± 19[a]	Halothane-O_2	Hildebrand and Howitt, 1984
Sheep	5.0 ± 0.61 0.15/min	21 ± 2.5 steady state	Halothane-O_2	Klein et al., 1985; Cass et al., 1980
Horse	82 ± 7.3	20-35	Halothane-O_2	Klein et al., 1983
Pony	125 ± 20[a]	16	Halothane-O_2	Manley et al., 1983
Pig	50		Thiopental-N_2O-O_2, or ketamine	Denny and Lucke, 1977
	10			Lumb and Jones, 1984
Dog	22 ± 3	108 ± 10	Halothane	Booij et al., 1980
Cat	20	15 ± 2[a]	Halothane-α-chloralose	Hughes and Chapple, 1976
	22	14 ± 2	Pentobarbital	Durant et al., 1980
	34	8.8 ± 2.3	α-Chloralose-pentobarbital	Durant et al., 1979

[a]Mean ± standard deviation.

SOURCE: Modified from Klein, 1987.

reference contains much useful information and it should be consulted by individuals considering the use of neuromuscular blocking agents in anesthetized animals.

The maintenance of a constant depth of anesthesia or general knowledge of the depth of anesthesia is especially important when neuromuscular blocking agents are used with light anesthesia. When a neuromuscular blocking agent is necessary, the general anesthesia to be used in a specific study should be administered to a nonparalyzed animal to an appropriate depth in a test situation before the neuromuscular agent is used, to determine the adequacy of the general anesthesia. Many signs of anesthesia are eliminated when muscle paralysis occurs, and delivery of an adequate depth of anesthesia is essential. Because of an animal's inability to respond to stimuli when paralyzed, it is difficult to evaluate whether the animal is anesthetized or can feel pain. Observable signs that might indicate pain under paralysis include autonomic nervous system changes such as lacrimation and salivation, sudden changes in heart rate and arterial blood pressure, and changes in pupil size. Any attempt to breathe out of synchrony with a ventilator might indicate a response to pain, lack of adequate anesthesia, inadequate ventilation (as reflected in increased arterial CO_2 concentration), or hypoxia. Those signs, either singly or in combination, can provide valuable information about an animal's condition, but they are not infallibly linked to the animal's state and should be used cautiously and validated separately for each experimental situation.

The following recommendations, adapted from Movshon (1988), might be helpful.

- Necessary surgical procedures should be performed under general surgical anesthesia and before the induction of paralysis. If such procedures might have painful consequences during the later paralysis, local anesthesia should be used in a manner shown by the experimenter to be effective over comparable periods after surgery in alert, freely moving animals of the same species. Endotracheal intubation and other preparatory procedures should take place under general anesthesia, as should the induction of paralysis.

- Fixation of an animal in any restraining device requires suitable implanted devices previously fitted under surgical anesthesia. Those are known to be well tolerated and to be neither painful nor stressful in awake, unparalyzed animals. Local anesthesia of pressure points is recommended. (Pressure points are parts of the body that become painful owing to continued application of pressure.)

- Other devices attached to the animal should be placed to provide maximal comfort. The pharynx and larynx should be treated with a topical anesthetic. The tracheal cannula should be coated with a lubricant that contains a local anesthetic agent and must be immobilized so that it cannot be moved inadvertently when general anesthesia has subsided. Intravenous catheters likewise must be immobilized.

- The animal should be placed in one of its natural resting positions. Minor adjustments in posture from time to time might be helpful in preventing pooling of blood in large veins.

- Salivation should be controlled with a suitable drug, or some other innocuous means should be used to prevent the accumulation of secretion in the throat.

- The duration of paralysis must be dictated by the time over which the physiologic condition of the animal, and hence its comfort and well-being, can readily be maintained. For most species that will not exceed about 4-6 hours. Some form of intravenous supplementation might be needed, as will cannulation of the bladder in some species (such as tree shrews) if emptying does not occur spontaneously.

- If an animal is to recover from the paralysis and re-establish its respiration, it should happen while the animal is under general anesthesia. The skilled use of chemical antidotes can ease the process of recovery so that anesthesia can be brief and light.

- No procedure should be undertaken in an unanesthetized paralyzed animal until it has been shown—when the animal is fully alert, unparalyzed, and capable of expressing its reactions—that an identical procedure elicits no sign of discomfort or distress. That specifically includes, but is not limited to, insertion or manipulation of recording or other devices; electric, chemical, or other stimulation; and the measurement of optical reflexes.

- In an otherwise comfortable situation, the principal source of stress that occurs in paralyzed humans (and therefore, presumably, animals) is the sense of respiratory distress that accompanies an increase in arterial Pa_{CO_2}. Therefore, end-tidal CO_2 should be continuously monitored with a reliable, calibrated instrument, and its concentration should be kept substantially below the 4.7% at which respiratory distress can begin. It should be understood that CO_2 monitors designed for use in humans typically do not accurately measure end-tidal CO_2 in smaller animals, because excessive gas mixing occurs in the sampling apparatus. Also, relatively short periods of artificial ventilation are often accompanied by blood-chemical and pulmonary-function changes that alter the normal relationship between end-tidal CO_2 and arterial Pa_{CO_2}. Regular direct measurement of arterial blood gases is an indispensable component of monitoring, and monitoring with a respiratory-gas analyzer alone is inadequate.

- The heart rate should be monitored. Preferably, a ratemeter sounds an alarm if heart rate is above or below its natural resting range. Indeed, once an immobilized animal has recovered from general anesthesia, the heart rate might provide the experimenter with a ready index of the animal's state; an increase due to a relatively innocuous stimulus provides some assurance that the animal is alert and is not experiencing a severe stress.

- Body temperature should be monitored and strictly maintained within the limits normal for resting animals of the species in question. Body temperature will fall gradually because of immobilization, and there should be provision for keeping the animal warm. But devices used for that purpose should be incapable of overheating to a point that causes dangerously high temperatures or uncomfortable heating of the skin.

• Provision should be made for the rapid and effective delivery of an anesthetic agent, in case an indication of pain or distress occurs and its cause cannot be immediately identified and rectified.

• If an animal is to be repeatedly subjected to experiments requiring the use of muscle relaxants, signs of specific aversion to the experimental setting should be taken as evidence that the precautions being used are not adequate, and the experiments should be discontinued until appropriate procedural changes are made.

Control of Pain in Nonmammalian Species

Pain and nociception have been studied extensively in mammals, but there are few reports on the presence or absence of pain perception in other animals. Several investigators have attempted to determine that insects can perceive pain, but have concluded that they probably do not (Wigglesworth, 1980; Eisemann et al., 1984; Fiorito, 1986). A working party at the Institute of Medical Ethics in London has examined the evidence that cephalopods might perceive pain (Smith and Morton, 1988). Cephalopods can be trained with negative reinforcers; they learn to escape and avoid noxious stimuli, and repeated noxious stimulation appears to have long-term effects on behavior. But there is very little evidence that would permit a conclusion that cephalopods perceive pain.

Attempts of cold-blooded vertebrates and invertebrates to escape or avoid aversive stimuli are not sufficient to conclude that these animals experience the affective and sensory qualities of painful stimuli as do warm-blooded vertebrates, but they do indicate that at least some degree of stress can be accompanied by a negative motivational state, and they should not be ignored. In the absence of contrary information, consideration should be given to alleviating and preventing potential pain and stress in cold-blooded vertebrates and invertebrates, as for warm-blooded vertebrates (Eisemann et al., 1984).

Fish have neuropeptides in their central nervous systems, such as substance P and enkephalin, that are similar to those in mammalian nociceptive systems. They respond to injury or irritants by withdrawing, but their responses to repeated stimuli are small or absent, and fish with severe wounds appear to behave normally. Therefore, it is difficult to describe the responses of fish to noxious stimuli as unequivocal signs of pain. Despite the lack of direct evidence that fish perceive pain as do other vertebrates (Medway, 1980; Arena and Richardson, 1990), it seems prudent at present to try to minimize pain in fish as in warm-blooded vertebrates.

Neonatal and Fetal Surgery

The traditional view that the human neonate and fetus are not capable of perceiving pain has recently been seriously questioned (Anand et al., 1987a). A review of the literature, including reports of animal experiments, showed that premature human fetuses and neonates indeed show physiologic and probably psychologic evidence of severe stress when subjected to surgical procedures that result in marked nociceptive activity. The authors concluded that "current knowledge suggests that humane considerations should apply as forcefully to the case of neonates and young, non-verbal infants as they do to children and adults in similar painful and stressful situations."

Drug regimens that are safe for and tolerated by adult animals and humans can produce toxicity or even death in neonates or fetuses. Protective mechanisms—including drug-biotransforming enzyme systems, the blood-brain barrier, and renal excretory mechanisms—are undeveloped in fetal and neonatal animals (Stoelting, 1987). We underscore the published recommendation that "the choice of methods to be used in neonates is another area in which the flexible cooperation of principal investigators and veterinarians is particularly important" (Van Sluyters and Oberdorfer, 1991).

Some general recommendations can be made: Consider the use of a local anesthetic when surgery is to be performed on a fetus. Consider the use of an inhaled anesthetic for neonates whenever possible, because biotransformation is not required for its elimination, and the depth of anesthesia can be readily controlled. Analgesia can be provided by using fentanyl in preterm human babies (Anand et al., 1987b).

NONPHARMACOLOGIC CONTROL OF PAIN

HYPOTHERMIA

One analgesic technique that is applicable to altricious neonates that have not yet developed effective thermoregulatory mechanisms is hypothermia, which has a wide margin of safety and appears to be effective when surgery is necessary. It is also useful for restraint and as an adjunct to general anesthesia in cold-blooded animals (CCAC, 1980; Phifer and Terry, 1986; Arena and Richardson, 1990).

TONIC IMMOBILITY

Physical restraint can produce severe stress in some animal species (Gärtner et al., 1980; Pare and Glavin, 1986). Such stress is usually accompanied by functional CNS changes and hormonal responses. In some highly susceptible species—such as reptiles, birds, guinea pigs, and rabbits—restraint can result, usually after an initial period of struggling, in immobility that persists without continued restraint. The most common terms for the phenomenon are *immobility reflex*, *animal hypnosis*, and *tonic immobility*. Tonic immobility (TI) is probably the least ambiguous, because it is more of a behavioral description. Other terms—such as *playing possum*, *mesmerism*, and *dead feint*—have been used. The reflexive behavior is considered to be a mechanism of defense against predators, in that it renders the animal less sensitive to pain. Those intending to use TI should consult

Klemm (1976) and Porro and Carli (1988) for rationale, technique, and species differences.

TI abolishes voluntary motor activity. Spinal reflexes are suppressed, but not abolished. Muscle tone varies with species and with the induction procedure. In rabbits, perhaps the most susceptible species, fine muscle tremors can occur initially or be induced by stimulation of the patellar tendon reflex. Rabbits' eyes remain open and fixed, but the corneal reflex is still present. Initially, the heart rate of immobilized animals can increase; at later stages, the rate tends to decrease. Fully immobilized rabbits exhibit pronounced catalepsy with reduced muscle tone.

In susceptible species, TI is relatively easy to achieve. A rabbit, for example, is grasped from behind around the neck at the base of the skull by one hand. With the other hand under the rump (and preventing kicking by the hind legs), the animal is turned over onto its back with one quick smooth motion while gentle traction is maintained on the neck. Gentle neck traction might stimulate receptors in the carotid body to play a role in the induction and maintenance of immobility. Rubbing the animal's abdomen and talking in a soft monotone are said to facilitate the reflex. An animal immobilized can commonly be left lying on its back for a short period without additional restraint. The reflex can last from a few seconds to several minutes; the period depends on the species, the animal, previous experience, and the time that the animal is held in the supine position. Gentle traction on its neck will continue maintenance of TI and its associated analgesia. Loud noises or sudden poking or probing of the animal will cause it to arouse.

TI is useful in performing physical examinations, deep abdominal palpation, and ophthalmologic examinations. It is readily reversible by returning the animal to its normal posture. After immobility is terminated, some degree of analgesia and disorientation can persist for a period that depends on the duration and depth of TI.

ACUPUNCTURE

The use of acupuncture is limited primarily to the treatment of specific chronic, painful disorders (Klide, 1989; Klide and Martin, 1989). It has been used successfully in the management of chronic pain in horses and dogs. It is not curative, and it has to be repeated periodically to allow the animal mobility and comfort.

Acupuncture has been successful in modifying acute pain, but has no lingering effect on removal of the stimulation. It has been used for surgical analgesia under limited circumstances.

6

Control of Stress and Distress

This chapter provides guidance on the control of stress and distress in laboratory animals *pharmacologically*—presenting information on the clinical uses, effects, and dosages of four groups of drugs (see Tables 6-1 and 6-2)—and *nonpharmacologically*.

Distress in laboratory animals is usually unnecessary and unwanted. Despite an inability to define or measure distress in laboratory animals precisely, *distress* is used to describe a point at which adaptation to a stressor (environmental, psychologic, or physiologic) is not sufficient to maintain equilibrium and maladaptive behaviors appear. Users of animals are responsible for the prevention, alleviation, or elimination of distress. The possibility of distress is best considered *before* laboratory animals are used experimentally; that is, careful consideration should be given during experimental design to means by which non-pain-induced distress can be avoided (ideally) or minimized. Stressors that can lead to distress should be understood and identified (see Chapter 3). If one is to deal adequately with distress in laboratory animals, one must be able to recognize it (see Chapter 4). That requires that species-typical behaviors associated with well-being be understood and that the normal behavior and appearance of the animals being used be known. Distress can be subtle; so too can its influence on experimental outcomes.

Distress results from stress to which animals cannot adequately adapt. The stressor can be an external or internal event that causes physical or psychologic trauma. For its purpose, the committee identified these stressors as pain-induced and environmentally induced. Nominal stress is usually cause for alarm only if an animal is unable to adapt properly to it. When that occurs and distress results, treatment should begin with an identification of the underlying cause. Pain-induced stress should then be alleviated by removal of the cause of the pain or through administration of analgesics, but non-pain-induced stress is seldom amenable to pharmacologic treatment alone. Rather, environmental stressors or factors should be addressed. The use of tranquilizers can sometimes help an animal adapt to necessary changes in its environment, but is seldom sufficient in itself.

This report places considerable emphasis on the importance of recognizing maladaptive behaviors resulting from stress with which an animal is unable to cope effectively as evidence of distress. Some conditions of acute stress in which an animal's behavior is normal and adaptive also suggest that intervention is warranted. Such conditions are brought on typically when an animal is strongly motivated to avoid or escape a stimulus or set of conditions. Such behaviors, like maladaptive ones, should be interpreted as causing harm to the animal and producing unwanted variability in research data.

PHARMACOLOGIC CONTROL OF STRESS AND DISTRESS

The tranquilizers and sedatives used in animals today include drugs in four groups: phenothiazines, butyrophenones, benzodiazepines, and α_2-adrenergic agonists. Phenothiazines and butyrophenones have many common properties, especially general sympatholytic activity. They used to be considered "major" tranquilizers in human medicine; currently preferred terms are *antipsychotics* and *neuroleptics*. Benzodiazepines, once considered "minor" tranquilizers, are now thought of as antianxiety-sedative agents. α_2-Adrenergic agonists have emerged as a very important group of drugs for tranquilizing and sedating animals.

PHENOTHIAZINES

Common Examples

Promazine (Sparine®) and acetylpromazine (Acepromazine®).

Clinical Use

Phenothiazines depress many physiologic functions, decrease motor activity, produce mental calming, and increase the threshold of response to environmental stimulation. Thus, they are useful for animal restraint. They do not produce sleep, analgesia, or anesthesia. The sedation produced by phenothiazines differs from the state produced by barbiturates and opioids, in that sedation occurs without hypnosis and the effects produced in animals can be reversed with an adequate stimulus.

In animals, adequate doses produce a quieting effect that includes sedation, ataxia, an increase in the threshold of response to environmental stimuli, relaxation of the nictitating membrane in some animals, and abolition of conditioned reflexes. It must be emphasized that animals under the sedation produced by tranquilizers can still react in a coordinated manner. A large animal can still kick with full force in reaction to painful stimuli, a vicious animal can still bite, and nonhuman primates can become aroused unexpectedly. The degree of sedation and inactivity produced by the tranquilizers in many instances depends on the excitability of the animal being treated. That is especially true in wild animals: the tranquilization of free-living and captive undomesticated animals might not be possible, and more potent drugs might be necessary (Graham-Jones, 1960, 1964). It is also true of vicious animals; i.e., tranquilizers might produce insufficient restraint for safe management of extremely high-strung nervous animals. In those circumstances, neuroleptanalgesia might have to be administered with a combination of a tranquilizer and an opioid. In stallions, many phenothiazine tranquilizers cause erections and temporary or permanent prolapse of the penis. In horses, phenothiazines and butyrophenones cause involuntary and hallucinatory activity (Muir et al., 1989).

Pharmacologic Effects

The major action of the phenothiazines is antagonism of the central dopamine receptors. In addition to their sedative properties, the phenothiazines and the related butyrophenones (e.g., droperidol) produce a dose-dependent decrease in motor activity. At greater doses, they produce a cataleptic state that includes rigidity, tremor, and akinesia. The phenothiazines are also useful in some species as antiemetics. However, they have important anticholinergic, antiadrenergic, and antihistaminic effects, which often lead to undesirable or unanticipated side effects and unpredictable drug interactions.

The two most commonly used phenothiazines are promazine and acetylpromazine. They produce numerous cardiovascular effects through central and peripheral actions on the sympathetic nervous system and the CNS and direct actions on vascular and cardiovascular smooth muscle. The CNS manifestation is inhibition of centrally mediated pressor reflexes, which reduces both vascular tone and the ability to respond reflexively to alterations in the cardiovascular system. The peripheral effects are related to α_2-adrenergic receptor blockade.

Phenothiazines are commonly administered intravenously to animals in the standing position, especially farm animals. The cardiovascular actions have a more rapid onset than the sedative actions, and orthostatic hypotension might explain the occasional collapse. The extent of hypotensive effects of a tranquilizer varies and depends on the state of the cardiovascular system and the sympathetic tone when the drug is administered. Fatigue, hypovolemia, excitement, and trauma can increase sympathetic tone as a part of the adaptive homeostatic process. The administration of a sympatholytic drug under those circumstances can have a profound effect (Bahga and Link, 1966). Phenothiazines lessen the ability of the cardiovascular system to compensate for changes in vascular volume, changes in position, and stress. They can produce hemodilution by causing splenic sequestration of red blood cells (Collette and Meriwether, 1965); the effect is especially noted in horses.

Dose Recommendations (Table 6-1)

Under some circumstances, phenothiazine doses that do not produce obvious overt behavioral manifestations (lower than those recommended in Table 6-1) could be used to alter behavioral patterns slightly and should be considered as adjuncts for the treatment of abnormal behaviors.

Phenothiazines are useful in managing postanesthetic emergence delirium, especially after barbiturate anesthesia. A combination of a tranquilizer and an

TABLE 6-1   Doses of Tranquilizers in Various Species

Species	Drug	Dose, mg/kg (Route[a])	Reference
Cat	Promazine	2.2-4.4 (iv, im)	Soma, 1971
	Acetylpromazine	0.03-0.05 (iv, im)	Gleed, 1987
Cattle	Promazine	0.4-1.1 (iv, im)	Soma, 1971
	Acetylpromazine	0.1 (im)	Gleed, 1987
Dog	Promazine	2.2-4.4 (iv, im)	Soma, 1971
	Acetylpromazine	0.03-0.05 (iv, im)	Gleed, 1987
Guinea pig	Promazine	0.5-1.0 (im)	CCAC, 1980
Hamster	Promazine	0.5-1.0 (im)	CCAC, 1980
Horse	Promazine	0.44-1.1 (iv, im)	Soma, 1971
	Acetylpromazine	0.02-0.05 (iv, im)	Gleed, 1987
Mouse	Promazine	5 (ip)	Vanderlip and Gilroy, 1981
	Acetylpromazine	2-5 (ip)	Flecknell, 1987
Primate	Acetylpromazine	0.2 (im)	Flecknell, 1987
Rabbit	Promazine	1-2 (im)	CCAC, 1980
	Acetylpromazine	1 (im)	McCormick and Ashworth, 1971
Rat	Promazine	0.5-1.0 (im)	Kruckenberg, 1979
	Acetylpromazine	1.0 (im)	Flecknell, 1987
Sheep and goat	Promazine	0.44-1.1 (iv, im)	Soma, 1971
	Acetylpromazine	0.04-0.06 (iv, im)	Soma, 1971
Swine	Acetylpromazine	1.1-2.2 (im)	Benson and Thurman, 1979

[a]iv = intravenous; im = intramuscular; ip = intraperitoneal.

opioid might facilitate management during the immediate postanesthetic and postoperative period.

BUTYROPHENONES

Common Examples

Azaperone (Stresnil®) and droperidol.

Clinical Use

Azaperone is approved for swine, in which it is used mainly to prevent fighting and as a preanesthetic agent. It is a more potent sedative and less hypotensive than the phenothiazines, but has no analgesic effect (Flecknell, 1987). Droperidol is incorporated with fentanyl in Innovar-Vet® (see Chapter 5).

Pharmacologic Effect

Like the phenothiazines, butyrophenones exert general sympatholytic activity that probably accounts for many of their common properties. Butyrophenones seem more likely to produce extrapyramidal signs of rigidity, tremors, and catalepsy.

Dose Recommendations

In pigs, azaperone at 2.2 mg/kg intramuscularly produces sedation, but has no analgesic effect. Combined at 5 mg/kg with metomidate (10 mg/kg) intramuscularly, it produces sedation and analgesia suitable for minor surgical procedures (Flecknell, 1987). In horses, azaperone administered intravenously at 0.22-0.44 mg/kg might cause excitement and extrapyramidal effects and is not recommended (Muir et al., 1989).

BENZODIAZEPINES

Common Examples

Diazepam (Valium®), zolazepam, and midazolam (Versed®).

Clinical Use

Benzodiazepines induce a mild calming effect and have therapeutically useful anticonvulsant, muscle-relaxant, and hypnotic effects in animals; they have no analgesic activity. They are commonly used with analgesic drugs (e.g., xylazine, opioids, or ketamine) to enhance muscle relaxation.

Pharmacologic Effects

Barbiturates and benzodiazepines share many pharmacologic actions (e.g., sedation, muscle relaxation, anticonvulsant activity, and hypnosis) because of their interaction with the GABA-chloride ionophore receptor complex. GABA (γ-aminobutyric acid) is an inhibitory amino acid neurotransmitter. Benzodiazepines appear to increase the frequency of opening of the GABA-activated chloride ion channel in nerve membranes; barbiturates enhance the binding of GABA to its receptor and increase the time that the same GABA-activated ion channel is open. Thus, barbiturates and benzodiazepines both facilitate GABA-mediated inhibitory effects on the CNS.

The sedative and anxiolytic effects of the benzodiazepines are produced by doses that also produce muscle relaxation. The most commonly used benzodiazepine is diazepam. As with other drugs, there is great species variability in its effects. The effects in dogs, cats, and horses (Muir et al., 1982) are not the anxiolytic effects noted in people. Excitement, tremors, ataxia, dysphasia, and sometimes sedation occur in animals. There is no known explanation for the major species differences noted in response to the benzodiazepines in people and animals.

Dose Recommendations

Diazepam, usually administered intravenously, is painful if given intramuscularly. In rats, it is used as an anxiolytic at 1 mg/kg to lessen stress-induced increases in blood pressure, but not changes in heart rate (Conahan and Vogel, 1986). It can be used in ruminants for sedation at 0.2-0.5 mg/kg. In small ruminants, it is used as a premedication before ketamine anesthesia.

Diazepam and midazolam are usually used with other drugs in animals. The water solubility of midazolam, as opposed to the water insolubility of diazepam (compounded with propylene glycol), might be advantageous in some drug combinations, and midazolam is less irritating to tissues. However, it is more expensive. Tables 5-4 and 5-5 list combinations of diazepam with ketamine for surgical anesthesia in several species. The preanesthetic administration of the benzodiazepines with ketamine provides good muscle relaxation and eliminates tremors produced by ketamine.

α_2-ADRENERGIC AGONISTS

Common Examples

Xylazine (Rompun®) and detomidine (Dormosedan®).

Clinical Uses

Xylazine is often used alone or with ketamine as a sedative and preanesthetic in ruminants and horses (Clarke and Hall, 1969; Hoffman, 1974; Klein and Baetjer,

1974; Klide et al., 1975; Muir et al., 1979). In horses and ponies, xylazine given alone produces a mild degree of CNS depression. There is some ataxia, but animals are able to stand and walk. Horses and ponies can still respond to painful stimuli, so surgical procedures should not be attempted without opioid supplementation or local analgesia. Xylazine suppresses the excitatory effects of opioids in horses when these drugs are administered together for analgesic or preanesthetic purposes.

Xylazine is used extensively in other species with other drugs, especially the dissociative anesthetic ketamine. Xylazine is not recommended for use alone to produce analgesia or anesthesia in dogs and cats, but is commonly used with ketamine. Vomiting occurs in dogs and cats after intravenous or intramuscular administration of xylazine (Klide et al., 1975), and sedative effects occur in dogs within 5-10 minutes of administration. Sedative effects include lying down, lack of response to the environment, medial rotation of the eyes, and prolapse of the nictitans. Some degree of analgesia is apparent, but xylazine is not sufficient for surgery. Spontaneous arousal can occur, and the degree of sedation is inconsistent.

Pharmacologic Effects

Xylazine is a potent adrenergic receptor α_2-agonist. The major CNS effect of the α_2-agonists is a decrease in sympathetic outflow from the medullary pressor center; this accounts for the sympatholytic actions of this class of drugs. Actions of xylazine at the central α_2-agonist adrenergic receptors produce a variety of effects, including sedation, analgesia, hypotension, bradycardia, hypothermia, mydriasis, and relief of anxiety. Cardiovascular changes in dogs and horses have been attributed to them (Klide et al., 1975; Muir et al., 1979). After intravenous administration of xylazine in dogs, heart rate and aortic flow decreased, blood-pressure changes were variable, and peripheral resistance increased; there were no significant changes in blood gases and pH; atrioventricular block and nonrespiratory sinus arrhythmia were seen; and atropine did not alter the changes in cardiac rhythm. Cardiovascular changes in horses were similar, except that a transient increase in blood pressure was followed by a decrease.

Other α_2-agonists have similar actions. Detomidine has recently been introduced in this country as Dormosedan® for use in horses. Detomidine (its intravenous and intramuscular dose is 0.02-0.04 mg/kg) is more potent than xylazine and can produce more profound analgesia, sedation, and bradycardia for a longer period (Kamerling et al., 1988).

Dose Recommendations (Tables 5-4, 5-5, and 6-2)

Dogs, cats, and ruminants (sheep, goats, and cattle) are more sensitive to xylazine than horses. Doses at the low end of the recommended range produce immobilization; recumbency can occur at higher doses (Table 6-2). Surgery is possible in depressed ruminants at 0.09-0.35 mg/kg. As with any agent that produces recumbency in ruminants, passive regurgitation can occur.

TABLE 6-2 Dose of Xylazine and Adjunctive Drugs Other Than Ketamine[a] in Various Species

Species	Dose, mg/kg (Route[b])	Adjunct Drug, mg/kg (Route[b])	Comments	References
Cat	1.1-4.4 (iv, im, sc)	None	Sedation, analgesia, emesis	Moye et al., 1973; Yates, 1973
Cattle	0.09-0.35 (im)	None	Sedation, analgesia	Hopkins, 1972
Dog	0.5-4.4 (iv, im, sc)	None	Sedation, analgesia, emesis	Moye et al., 1973; Yates, 1973; Klide et al., 1975
Horse	0.5-1.0 (iv, im)	None	Sedation	Hoffman, 1974
Horse	0.5-1.0 (iv, im)	Morphine, 0.2-0.5 (iv, im)	Sedation, analgesia	Klein and Baetjer, 1974
Horse	0.1-0.5 (iv)	Butorphanol, 0.01-0.04 (iv)	Preanesthesia restraint	Orsini, 1988
Rabbit	5.0 (sc)	Pentobarbital, 11-28 (iv)	Anesthesia	Hobbs et al., 1991

[a]Tables 5-4 and 5-5 list doses for xylazine in combination with ketamine.
[b]iv = intravenous; im = intramuscular; sc = subcutaneous.

NONPHARMACOLOGIC CONTROL OF STRESS AND DISTRESS

This section considers nonpharmacologic ways of preventing, minimizing, and alleviating non-pain-induced distress in laboratory animals through husbandry and management practices, socialization and handling, environmental enrichment, and experimental design. (The pharmacologic management of pain, a major stress that often leads to distress, is discussed in Chapter 5 and will not be discussed here, except to emphasize that the use of drugs to alleviate non-pain-induced distress is generally inappropriate.) As a general rule, nonpharmacologic approaches to the prevention or minimization of distress are more desirable than pharmacologic approaches (Wolfle, 1987).

HUSBANDRY AND MANAGEMENT PRACTICES

Control of non-pain-induced distress centers around three of the most common causes in laboratory animals: husbandry, environment, and experimental design.

Management practices in animal care and housing can contribute to such stressors as fear, anxiety, loneliness, and boredom, which, if not prevented or minimized, have the potential to lead to distress and the appearance of maladaptive behaviors. Hence, understanding and meeting the social and physical needs of animals are essential to the prevention or minimization of distress. Table 4-4 identifies situations and practices that can contribute to distress and adversely affect an animal's well-being. Two points require emphasis: a state of well-being is more than just good health and the absence of pain, and needs are species-specific.

It is helpful to keep in mind that no environment is free of stressors. Furthermore, even if a stress-free environment could be achieved, it would not necessarily be desirable. Stress is not always abnormal or harmful to well-being. Stressors are common in the lives of animals in their natural environments, and a captive animal that had never experienced stress would be quite different in its behavior and physiology from the typical members of its species.

Whether stress will lead to distress, with the appearance of maladaptive behaviors and physiologic and pathologic changes, and create a serious risk to an animal's well-being depends on the intensity and duration of the stress and the animal's adaptability. Rather than strive to keep a captive environment free of stressors, it is more realistic, and will serve animals' interests better, to try to identify and eliminate extreme forms of chronic or acute stress. That can be achieved partly by designing the physical environment, caretaking regimens, and research procedures from the animals' perspective. It is also helpful to consider the kinds of experiences that animals can be given to help them cope with stressors in situations they are likely to encounter in a captive setting.

Animal-centered approaches to stress and distress are essential, but they can easily be carried to an extreme. There are no animal utopias in nature or in artificial environments. No environments are entirely animal-centered. Even if they were, the biologic makeup of animals includes paradoxes and contradictions that environmental conditions cannot fully resolve. The assumption that animals "know what is best" for them is a charming fiction. The various activities they engage in, the goals they seek to reach, and the functions they carry out do not necessarily constitute a coherent, harmonious, and entirely beneficial whole; more often, they reflect compromises within the individual between conflicting or incompatible needs and tendencies. Some of the compromises can actually be potent sources of stress and can lead to distress. That is likely to be the case, for example, for both mother and offspring in many nonhuman primate species during the period surrounding weaning. The weaning process can, in fact, be so stressful that it increases the infant's vulnerability. Other examples can be found in Chapter 3.

Even if measures of stress and distress were wholly objective, concordant, and unequivocal, that would not always provide sufficient information on which to base practical decisions. One price of human stewardship, even if animal well-being were the only concern, is that human knowledge and human values necessarily influence the decision-making process. When data are lacking, purely anthropomorphic considerations are often helpful, if they are based on a solid understanding of the behavior of the species and the context. In some contexts, humans might make decisions that animals themselves would make, as is often the case between human parents and children. To ensure that decisions are as humane as possible, more information on the sources and manifestations of stress and distress in captive environments is helpful. Agreed-on guidelines for the identification and reduction of stress and the prevention and minimization of distress can also serve a useful purpose. In the pursuit of humane concerns, however, it is essential to recognize the need for professional judgment and to preserve as much flexibility as possible in the process by which practical decisions are reached and implemented.

The solutions to most of the problems concerning environmental sources of stress and distress in captive animals will eventually be provided by research. In the meantime, it is necessary to be sensitive to signs of stress and to take whatever steps are possible to control them—not only on humane grounds, but also because of the impact of stress on reproduction and research results. Animals that are chronically stressed are altered behaviorally and physiologically to the extent that they can experience reproductive failure.

Knowing the species being used and being familiar with the normal appearance and behavior of individual animals are the best preparation for detecting signs of stress and distress (Chapter 4). The next step is to determine their source. Except for pain and illness, stress, and distress in captive environments usually result from some degree of encroachment of the six ecologic dimensions (described in Chapter 3) on species-typical needs and behavioral tendencies. Those dimensions should be considered in designing captive environments and in planning management procedures, and they should be evaluated when conditions appear to be causing unacceptable stress.

Husbandry practices that contribute to distress should be corrected. The environment should be well defined and controlled (e.g., established temperature, humidity, ventilation, and illumination standards should be met, noise reduced, etc.). The housing, feeding, and care of laboratory animals should be appropriate for the species to promote their health and well-being. Personnel that care for and use animals should be adequately trained. Generally, these issues are not a major source of disagreement. The attainment of well-being, however, might require consideration of other factors, such as environmental enrichment and socialization.

Given the present state of knowledge, specific recommendations and guidelines are necessarily tentative. It is possible, however, to indicate the kinds of questions that are reasonable to consider when evaluating environmental sources of stress and distress that can be addressed through changes in husbandry practices. With the discussion of the six ecologic dimensions in Chapter 3 as a guide, we offer the following questions as examples for use in assessing the adequacy of husbandry practices.

Relationships with Conspecifics

- Should the animal be housed alone or with others?
- Does the animal belong to a species that is mainly solitary (such as cats) or that normally lives in social groups (such as dogs, nonhuman primates, and most rodents)?
- Is the animal is housed with others, is continuous group living characteristic of the species (such as sheep), or are seasonal or other cyclic variations in sociability the rule (such as hamsters)?
- If animals are housed in groups, are the number of animals and available space such as to prevent crowding?
- Are the members of the group compatible? Are some animals being picked on or always causing trouble?
- Are the numbers or proportions of adult males, adult females, and immature animals in the group appropriate?
- Have all members of the group been adequately socialized with conspecifics during their early development?
- Are the animals familiar with each other?
- Is fighting or aggressive dominance a normal feature of social relationships in the species? If so, are physical arrangements—such as the volume of space, the location of barriers, and the placement of food sources—appropriate to minimize aggression?
- If offspring are to be separated from parents, when should this occur, which sex normally leaves the family group, and at what age? What provisions have been made to keep stress from becoming extreme?

Predator-Prey Relationships

• Is the individual in a species that normally relies on other animals as a source of food?

• If the species is predatory, what is its normal mode of capturing prey and what stimuli are likely to elicit this behavior?

• Are there any indications that the elicitation and frustration of predatory behaviors is an important significant source of stress or distress?

• Should steps be taken to reduce or control the stimulation of predatory behaviors?

• Are there frequent or chronic signs of defensive reactions, such as snarling, hissing, biting, cowering, and trembling?

• What events or environmental conditions usually produce defensive reactions?

• Have changes in physical arrangements, caretaking, or experimental procedures that might reduce defensive reactions been considered?

Shelter

• Is the animal in a species that normally uses shelters, dens, or cover?

• What functions do shelters, dens, and cover normally serve for the species (e.g., protection from elements or from predators or a depository for young)?

• If shelters, dens, and cover are provided in the captive environment, what purposes are they expected to serve? Are they adequately designed to fulfill these purposes?

• Is sanitation a problem?

• Does it appear that the animal's behavior is altered by the presence of shelters, dens, or cover so as to make it more fearful or more difficult to handle or to cause other effects that are undesirable from the standpoint of management and well-being?

• Does the animal scent-mark? If so, is this considered in the provisions for sanitation of the cage?

Spatial Architecture (Volume, Structure, and Topography)

• Does the volume of space meet the standards for the species recommended by the *Guide for the Care and Use of Laboratory Animals* (NRC, 1985) and the Animal Welfare Regulations (CFR Title 9)?

• How much of the available space is actually used by the animal, and how is it used?

• Does the animal display repetitive and stereotyped motor patterns or other behaviors that point to some inadequacy?

• Can caging arrangements be improved by adding perches, climbing devices, or other structures?

• Will such additions be consistent with the requirements of animal safety, restraint, and sanitation?

• If cages of different sizes or containing different kinds of equipment are in use, do they appear to have different effects on signs of stress and distress?

Feeding and Foraging Patterns

• Is the animal's food consistent in amount and quality with recommended standards for the species?

• What is the normal feeding pattern of the species?

• Do animals normally meet their nutritional requirements in a single meal with long intervals between feedings, eat intermittently throughout the day, or show some other predictable pattern?

• Are animals characteristically picky or wasteful feeders? Do they accept standard foods readily and consume them completely? How do they respond to unfamiliar foods?

• Is intake of the provided food adequate to maintain animals at an appropriate weight and in good health?

• Is searching for or preparing foods an important part of the normal activity of the species?

• Are there indications that animals attempt to engage in food-searching activities in the captive environment, even though they have no need to do so?

• Should feeding and foraging be facilitated by providing special opportunities, or can they be ignored without producing undesirable consequences?

• Within practical limitations, is the established feeding regimen consistent with the animal's preferred feeding patterns, with respect to scheduling and the kinds and amounts of food that are provided?

Environmental Events

Novelty, predictability, and control:

• What events in the captive environment are unpredictable (for example, light cycle, noise, and restraint)?

• Do any of those events seem to cause stress or distress?

• If practical steps can be taken to increase the animal's ability to predict those events, what effect is this likely to have on stress or distress?

• What procedures place the animal in a situation in which it is helpless, is coerced, or loses control over its own behavior (for example, restraint)?

• What practical steps can be taken to reduce stress and distress caused by such procedures (for example, adaptation with positive reinforcement and personnel training)?

• Is the animal in a species that characteristically shows high levels of spontaneous activity, interacts vigorously and flexibly with its surroundings, and appears curious about moderately novel objects and events (for example, dogs, rodents, and most nonhuman primates)?

• Does the animal appear to be listless, apathetic, or behaviorally depressed, compared with other members of its species and in the absence of any signs of ill health?

• Should enrichment devices or socialization be considered?

• If an enrichment device is used, what needs or behavioral tendencies is it designed to meet?

• Is the enrichment device consistent with the requirements of animal safety and sanitation?

• Is the enrichment device economical to construct, install, and maintain?

• Is the enrichment device actually used by the animal? In what way? How frequently? Under what conditions?

• What are the indications that the enrichment device contributes to well-being?

• Is the animal in a species that benefits from socialization with people?

SOCIALIZATION AND HANDLING

Socialization is achieved through conspecific housing or through interaction with other species, including humans. The benefit to any individual animal, however, should be carefully evaluated before pair-housing is implemented or an animal is introduced to a group, and a suitable period and method of adaptation should be provided. Many laboratory animals benefit from interaction with people, but this should be undertaken with due consideration for the animal's experience and zoonotic potential. There is general agreement about the value of conspecific socialization for the well-being of most laboratory animals, although it is not always easily achieved, because of the requirements of the protocol, space, finances, and other constraints.

It is well known that dogs respond favorably to direct interaction with humans and that their well-being can be enhanced by social, conspecific housing of compatible dogs. Socialization of puppies to humans and continued interaction with them might be the most stress-relieving practice for dogs. Human socialization should be included in every dog breeding program and stipulated in contracts for the purchase of dogs for research. Nonhuman primates might receive the greatest benefit from socialization with conspecifics, but direct human interaction can be beneficial under some circumstances, especially for an animal that is immature and singly housed. A predictable cause of maladaptive behaviors in nonhuman primates is social isolation when they are young. If early maternal separation is necessary, young primates will benefit from frequent exposure to cagemates. Continuous housing of very young animals together is not advisable, however, because it produces excessive mutual clinging and emotional dependence that impairs well-being and impedes normal social development. Where possible, infant nonhuman primates should be raised, at least through weaning, with their biologic mothers in a stable, species-typical social group in a predictable environment. Conspecific housing of incompatible animals and frequent changes in group composition lead to socially induced stress. Technicians responsible for the day-to-day care of nonhuman primates should not only understand the social behaviors of the species for which they are responsible, but also understand their role in maintaining social stability and controlling stress within and between cages or pens.

There is a substantial literature on the effect of human handling on the physiology, behavior, and development of various animals (Newton and Levine, 1968). The effects of handling are influenced by an animal's age and genotype and by the duration and frequency of handling. Most information has been obtained on laboratory rats. Handling pups between birth and weaning has been reported to have effects on many characteristics, including rate of growth and weight gain, learning, exploratory behavior, emotionality, physiology, responses to food and water deprivation, and the occurrence of some diseases or pathogens (Ader, 1967; Denenberg, 1969; Daly, 1973). Handling rats after weaning tends to be less effective. Comparable data on other species are lacking, but there are good reasons to assume that early handling, aimed at gentling animals and accustoming them to contact with humans, is likely to improve the docility and adaptability (and thus decrease stress) of most laboratory animals.

ENVIRONMENTAL ENRICHMENT

As defined in Chapter 1, the well-being of an animal encompasses more than freedom from pain and distress and is evaluated not just on the basis of growth and reproductive records, but from a global perspective of behavioral and physiologic stability. Because many stressors are of environmental origin, it is often assumed that the well-being of laboratory animals can be improved by environmental enrichment that permits animals an opportunity to express species-typical behaviors. Laboratory animals given the opportunity to perform species-typical behaviors may interact voluntarily with the enriched environment and participate in activities whose cessation could be interpreted as a change in well-being.

Enrichment devices and environmental changes to promote well-being of nonhuman primates are being studied extensively. However, what is appropriate for nonhuman primates (and other species) is a matter of some debate, and research is needed to determine which methods actually improve animal well-being (Beaver, 1989). For example, it is assumed that the creation of a more naturalistic environment for nonhuman primates will permit the expression of the normal range of behaviors. But there is some uncertainty about the validity of the assumption, because it has been reported that the "naturalness" of the environment is not as important to an animal's well-being as are events that are arranged to be contingent on the animal's behavior. Feeding puzzles, manipulanda, and artificial appliances with which the animals can interact encourage investigation and activity and are generally acknowledged to enrich the environment (see Beaver, 1989).

Although attention is being focused on nonhuman primates, methods for environmental enrichment of other species should be evaluated. Concentration on enrichment of the environment by incorporating objects or devices within the cage should cause the extreme importance of social interaction, possibly the most important form of enrichment for most laboratory animals, to be ignored. The proper balance between conspecific and human social interaction, a cage and room environment developed with an understanding of the normal behaviors of the species, and caring personnel trained to handle and care for the species should be the goal.

EXPERIMENTAL DESIGN

The objectives of some experiments require the production of stress or even distress (e.g., through food and water deprivation, maternal deprivation, social isolation, etc.), and investigators should be sensitive to the ethical concerns raised by such objectives. Experiments should be justified, use the minimal number of animals consistent with an effective design and statistical analyses, and minimize the duration and magnitude of stress. Restriction of food intake to develop appropriate reward-motivated behaviors in behavioral studies, usually in rats, is common. In those experiments, rats are usually maintained at about 80% of their ad libitum feeding weight, which is considered neither unethical nor excessive deprivation. Although novel foods might be used as environmental enrichment (Chapter 3), the response to novel foods, in either an experimental or a husbandry context, can be stressful. Foods usually should not be changed in the course of an experiment.

Caging conditions (e.g., single housing of rodents) and restraint (e.g., of rodents and nonhuman primates) produce stress, which can be so extreme or prolonged that an animal is unable to adapt and becomes distressed and maladaptive. Those procedures often can be minimized by handling and appropriate adaptation procedures, respectively. Because the novelty of an experience increases an animal's emotional response to it, habituating laboratory animals to experimental procedures by regular handling and adaptation to potentially stress-producing procedures should be incorporated into experimental protocols. For example, stress is associated with the first experience of dogs introduced to the leash, monkeys restrained in a chair, or cage-reared rats removed from their cage. Whether the stress of those experiences manifests itself in maladaptive behaviors (e.g., twirling on the leash, self-mutilation in the chair, or freezing and immobility, respectively) and thus distress will likely depend on factors external to the procedures themselves, such as previous experiences of the animal that led to expectations of pleasure or stress, familiarity with people, development of coping strategies for other events, and even time of day. Likewise, the biologically adaptive response to stressful stimuli has been shown to be subject to the early experience of the animal (Melzack and Scott, 1957; Green, 1978). Adaptation and handling to minimize stress and prevent distress can be applied to many experimental settings and procedures: chair restraining of nonhuman primates (when necessary for short periods) should be preceded by a series of brief introductions to the chair by a familiar person and rewarded by favorite foods either in the chair or immediately on returning to the home cage. Movement of animals to test chambers or laboratories should be preceded by several days or weeks of conditioning trips in which no aversive interaction takes place and food reward is provided. Through such means, a "transfer cage" or leash can signal a pleasurable event for the animal and facilitate a difficult task for the responsible person. In each case, the goal should be the positive association of the desired task favorably with a conditioned stimulus, such as the transfer cage, leash, or familiar technician. The stimulus need not always be a physical entity; the time of day or the ring of a bell can come to convey the same information, if presented in a predictable and routine manner and associated with the event to which the animal is being adapted. Adaptation to strange or unusual objects or environments, before the experimental introduction of the animal to the object or environment, reduces the novelty and stress of the experience and the likelihood that it will affect the experimental results.

Other experimental procedures and poor or inappropriate techniques, such as those common in blood withdrawal or antibody production, also can lead to stress. Amyx (1987) summarized procedures for antibody production, emphasizing that a reduction in volumes injected and a change in the site of injection minimizes the pain and distress of immunization procedures. Distress can be further minimized by sedative pretreatment, rather than use of restrainers. Blood withdrawal can lead to stress if the amount removed exceeds 1% of the animal's body weight.

Adaptation and socialization are strategies for reducing the distress of laboratory animals, preventing or alleviating distress, and thereby enhancing their well-being.

7

Euthanasia

GENERAL CONSIDERATIONS

Euthanasia is the act of inducing death without pain. Humane death of an animal may be defined as one in which the animal is rendered unconscious, and thus insensitive to pain, as rapidly as possible with a minimum of fear and anxiety.

The *1986 Report of the AVMA Panel on Euthanasia* (AVMA, 1986) is a comprehensive review of euthanasia, and persons involved in euthanasia of animals should refer to it. (The AVMA panel report is being revised.) This chapter will not duplicate the AVMA report, but will summarize and supplement it with emphasis on animals used in research, teaching, and testing.

EUTHANASIA AS AN OPTION FOR ALLEVIATION OF PAIN

Euthanasia is an acceptable method for relieving pain or distress that cannot be controlled by other means. For studies in which death of the animal can be anticipated or is an inevitable part of the protocol, the investigator should specify the end point of the experiment and alternative situations in which termination of the experiment would be mandatory to avoid distress. Such specifications may be based on pathologic, physiologic, or behavioral considerations. Unless euthanasia would interfere with the experimental protocol, animals should be humanely killed*

---

*Following the convention of the *1986 Report of the AVMA Panel on Euthanasia*, the verb *euthanatize* is used in this report. Other acceptable terms are *euthanasia* and *humanely kill*, but not *put to sleep*, *put down*, or other common euphemisms.

when death is certain or predictable, before they become moribund, rather than allowed to die and possibly be cannibalized by cagemates or allowed to undergo autolysis. Tissue autolysis, especially in rodents and other small mammals, can reduce the opportunity to evaluate some aspects of a study. Euthanasia can avoid or terminate unnecessary and severe pain and distress and allow for a complete necropsy. Developing uniform methods to assess morbidity as part of the protocol can contribute to the validity and uniformity of experimental data.

Regardless of the cause of morbidity (i.e., spontaneous or experimentally induced illness, pain, or distress), euthanasia should be considered. No guidelines are available that provide specific information on when to euthanatize animals in pain or distress, and such guidelines would be unrealistic, because animal species, types of studies, experimental needs, and end points vary so widely. Nevertheless, for studies in which death of animals is a necessary part of the protocol, efforts should be made to determine an acceptable end point when euthanasia may be performed to prevent or minimize unnecessary prolongation of pain and distress.

WHEN TO PERFORM EUTHANASIA

Some factors to consider in deciding whether to perform euthanasia are weight loss; emaciation; failure to gain weight (in a growing animal); severe pain that cannot be controlled; inordinate tumor growth or ascites; prolonged self-trauma; generalized alopecia caused by disease; prolonged diarrhea for which treatment is precluded in the protocol; coughing, wheezing, or severe nasal discharge; shallow and labored breathing; prolonged lethargy associated with rough hair coat, hunched posture, abdominal distention, or impaired movement; severe anemia or leukemia; icterus; CNS signs, such as convulsions, paralysis, paresis, tremors, and progressive head tilt; uncontrolled hemorrhage; urinary dysfunction (polyuria or anuria); lesions that interfere with eating or drinking; infectious disease (in terminal phases); hypothermia; and impairment of function, disablement, and other behavioral and physiologic signs of distress.

Information on signs of pain, distress, morbidity, and moribund condition in previous chapters of this volume should be used to determine when euthanasia is appropriate and justified. Another factor in the decision is the differentiation between a condition from which animals might recover and a moribund condition that is likely to progress to death. Principal investigators, study directors, attending veterinarians, and institutional animal care and use committees (IACUCs) should collaborate in determining general policies regarding end points of studies and when to perform euthanasia. In specific instances when euthanasia should be considered for humane reasons, attending veterinarians should consult with principal investigators and study directors in making a final decision. The IACUC at the University of Texas M. D. Anderson Cancer Center has considered this issue for rats and mice used in the center's programs (Tomasovic et al., 1988). Such guidelines, applied case by case, provide a rationale for determining whether potentially lethal experiments are justified in accordance with institutional policy and the merits of the research.

AESTHETICS OF EUTHANASIA: TRAINING, SKILL, AND EMOTIONAL IMPACT ON PEOPLE

Objective information on euthanasia of animals is sparse. Much of the information on the effects of the various agents and methods is subjective and based on professional judgment, experience, and intuition. Some of the reported disadvantages and arguments against particular practices are based in part on sentiment and human aesthetic considerations, rather than sound scientific data (Lumb, 1974). Some physical methods are aesthetically unpleasant but quite humane. Because unconsciousness and death do not necessarily occur simultaneously, it might be difficult for an untrained attendant to determine whether an animal is in distress or is unconscious and vocalizing and moving involuntarily without pain. Although the choice of a means of euthanasia should be based on humane concern for the animal being killed, the sensitivity of the attendant and observers should not be dismissed. Those performing or observing euthanasia can experience stress. People's emotions regarding this matter vary, and co-workers should be empathetic and sensitive to their feelings and attitudes. The possible necessity for euthanasia and untoward situations that might require euthanasia should be included in protocols and should be planned for and discussed among all personnel involved. Supportive discussion groups led by persons knowledgeable about grief and death can be useful in dealing with this difficult procedure (CCAC, 1980; Owens et al., 1981; Bustad, 1982; Wolfle, 1985; Arluke, 1990).

Euthanasia should be conducted professionally and compassionately by skilled persons using means that are optimal for the circumstances. Persons performing euthanasia should verify that the animals presented are those scheduled for euthanasia. When properly performed by competent persons using appropriate techniques, euthanasia is humane. However, if inappropriate procedures are used or personnel are incompetent, attempts at euthanasia can result in inhumane treatment of animals. Therefore, it is imperative that IACUCs and attending veterinarians provide for the training of personnel who will perform euthanasia and carefully monitor the procedures.

RESEARCH CONSIDERATIONS

Well-designed objective studies of euthanasia are needed and recommended. The assessment tools and measures to be considered for such studies include electroencephalograms, electrocardiograms, electromyograms, arterial blood pressure, respiration and heart rates, serum biochemical characteristics, pupil diameter, and behavior. Although decapitation is considered by many knowledgeable persons to produce instantaneous unconsciousness and death (Allred and Berntson, 1986; Vanderwolf et al., 1988), just how quickly death by decapitation occurs has been questioned (Mikeska and Klemm, 1975). Recommendations for sedation of all animals before decapitation, unless the head will be immediately frozen in liquid nitrogen (AVMA, 1986), are controversial. Decapitation below the level of the atlanto-occipital joint should be avoided, because it fails to interrupt all afferent fibers. If restraint is a problem or one is not confident that severance will be above this level, prior sedation is recommended.

AVOIDING FEAR IN OTHER ANIMALS

Distress vocalizations, fearful behavior, and release of odors or pheromones by a frightened animal can cause anxiety and apprehension in other animals (AVMA, 1986). That can affect the well-being of nearby animals and the validity of experimental data on animals to be euthanatized later by compromising their physiologic stability. Therefore, it is recommended that, whenever possible, animals be euthanatized in an area separated from other live animals, especially of their own species.

ADJUNCTS TO EUTHANASIA

Relief of pain and distress is of primary concern during the euthanasia procedure, so it might be necessary to administer drugs other than those used expressly for euthanasia, especially to nervous or intractable animals. Thus, tranquilizers, analgesics, or narcotics may be given before euthanasia to minimize apprehension and assist in animal control.

VERIFICATION OF DEATH

It is imperative that death be verified. Proper techniques of euthanasia should include a followup examination to confirm the absence of a heartbeat, which is a reliable indicator of death. Monitoring respiration is not sufficient. In some animals, particularly under deep CO_2 anesthesia, heartbeat can be maintained after visible respiration has ceased, and the animal might eventually recover.

SELECTION OF EUTHANATIZING AGENTS AND METHODS

A means of euthanasia is chosen on the basis of animal species, size, tractability, excitability, presence of painful injury, distress, disease, restraint of the animal, protocol requirements for tissue collection or analysis, and other considerations. Suitable physical control of the animal being killed is critical for satisfactory euthanasia to minimize fear, anxiety, and pain and to ensure the safety of attending persons and other nearby persons and animals. The selection of a procedure also depends on the skill of the personnel performing euthanasia and the number of animals to be killed.

The criteria that should be used in selecting an agent or method for euthanasia include:

- Lack of pain perception by the animal.
- Relative rapidity and irreversibility.
- Minimal stress, apprehension, and fear in the animal or in nearby animals.
- Minimal interference with experimental protocol.
- Simultaneous interruption of consciousness and reflex mechanisms.
- Safety of personnel.
- Reliability.
- Efficiency and ease of procedure.
- Cost and availability.
- Minimal psychologic stress for attending personnel and observers.
- Minimal adverse environmental impact.
- Minimal potential for human drug abuse.

Each means of euthanasia has advantages and disadvantages. It is unlikely that any agent or method will meet all the above criteria in a given situation.

An acceptable means of euthanasia must have an initial depressant action on the CNS that causes relatively rapid unconsciousness and insensitivity to pain. Therefore, an overdose of a chemical anesthetic is a desirable means of euthanasia. Once the animal is anesthetized, the method used to kill it is less important. In some research protocols, the use of chemical agents is contraindicated, and physical methods must be used.

When the animal is unconscious, it is desirable to stop its heart action as soon as possible, to reduce the flow of blood to its brain. A technique need not be considered inhumane merely because the heartbeat persists for a longer period, as long as the animal is unconscious (CCAC, 1980). There are three basic causes of death: hypoxia, either direct or indirect; direct depression of neurons vital for life functions; and damage to brain tissue (Sawyer, 1988).

Attitudes, sensitivities, and scientific knowledge regarding euthanasia are changing. A number of agents or methods formerly used are now considered undesirable, because they are inhumane, dangerous to personnel, or unaesthetic. Use of strychnine, nicotine, magnesium sulfate, potassium hydrochloride, hydrocyanic acid, curare, or succinylcholine is not considered acceptable (Lumb and Moreland, 1982). Others have sufficient disadvantages to exclude them from a list of recommended agents and methods.

Agents and methods recommended for euthanasia (Table 7-1) can be grouped into three categories: inhalational agents, physical methods, and noninhalational pharmacologic agents. The selection of the appropriate technique depends on an evaluation of the factors and criteria previously discussed.

TABLE 7-1 General Recommendations for Euthanasia (*Categorized by Agent*)

Agent or Method	Suitable Species	Remarks
Carbon dioxide	Small laboratory animals, small dogs and puppies, cats and kittens, birds, small swine, and terrestrial reptiles and amphibians	Not recommended for newborn animals
Barbiturates	Most species	Agent of choice
Methoxyflurane and halothane	Most laboratory animals	Expensive
Stunning	Small laboratory animals, snakes, lizards, turtles, terrapins, tortoises, frogs, toads, newts, salamanders, and fish	Follow by immediate killing
Cervical dislocation	Small laboratory animals	
Decapitation	Rodents and birds	Aesthetically unpleasant and dangerous for operator
Captive bolt	Large farm animals	Follow by immediate killing
Gunshot	Large animals and crocodilians	Useful in field studies, on farms, and in emergencies
Microwave irradiation	Mice and rats	Requires focused-beam instrument; expensive
Tricaine methanesulfate	Frogs, toads, newts, salamanders, and fish	

INHALATIONAL AGENTS

A number of inhalational agents have been used for euthanasia, including ether, chloroform, halothane, methoxyflurane, enflurane, isoflurane, cyclopropane, nitrous oxide, and the nonanesthetic gases carbon monoxide (CO), carbon dioxide (CO_2), nitrogen, argon, and hydrogen cyanide. Inhalational agents are usually administered in closed containers or chambers and have been used for small animals, such as rodents, rabbits, birds, puppies, kittens, and cats. Adequate ventilation and a means of exhausting waste gases should be provided for the safety of attendants using these agents.

The replacement of air with nonanesthetic gases produces a deficiency of available oxygen, and animals develop hypoxia. Without sufficient oxygen, the brain becomes depressed, and the animals lapse into unconsciousness. These gases are not recommended for euthanasia of newborn animals, because newborn animals have been accustomed to low oxygen concentration in the uterus and are more resistant to hypoxic conditions (Rowsell, 1981).

Although some of the agents have been widely used, most have sufficient disadvantages that preclude their common use for euthanasia of laboratory animals. Two disadvantages in some instances are that excitement and struggling are associated with the initial action on the CNS and initiating vapors can cause anxiety during induction.

Most of the agents are hazardous to attending personnel and other animals (AVMA, 1986). Halothane, methoxyflurane, enflurane, and isoflurane are expensive and thus impractical for routine use. Ether is explosive and therefore not recommended. Carcasses of animals killed by ether require special storage, handling, and disposal, because ether fumes are retained in the bodies. Chloroform should not be used, because it is extremely hepatotoxic and potentially carcinogenic for humans. Nitrous oxide alone is not potent enough to be useful. Hydrogen cyanide and CO are dangerous to personnel and are not recommended.

Carbon Dioxide

CO_2 is a well-accepted, commonly used gas for euthanasia of laboratory animals other than newborns. Inhalation of at least 40% CO_2 has a rapid anesthetic effect that proceeds to respiratory arrest and death if exposure is prolonged. It is effective for use in small laboratory animals, including rodents, rabbits, cats, poultry, small dogs, and swine. It is rapid, painless, humane, easy to use, relatively inexpensive, nonflammable, nonexplosive, nearly odorless, and heavier than air. If used in well-ventilated areas, it is much safer than most of the other inhalational agents. Waste gas poses no substantial environmental hazard. CO_2 is available in cylinders as a compressed gas or in a solid state as "dry ice." The compressed-gas form is preferable. Animals should be kept out of direct contact with dry ice, to prevent chilling or freezing. CO_2 is heavier than air, so chambers used for euthanasia should be filled from the bottom. Anxiety and struggling are minimized if the chamber is precharged. Relatively slow introduction of the gas into the chamber tends to minimize animal anxiety; high-speed flow causes turbulence and noise. Animals typically become unconscious within 45-60 seconds of the beginning of CO_2 exposure. With continued depression of vital centers, hypoxia and death occur soon. Animals should remain in the chamber for at least 5 or 6 minutes and then examined closely to determine that all vital signs have ceased before they are removed from the chamber and disposed of.

Consideration of Behavior

Burrowing animals, such as most rodents, tend to keep their noses in the lower portion of the chamber. Thus, narcosis, anesthesia, and death are relatively rapid when CO_2 is used. Investigative animals, such as dogs and rabbits, might extend their heads upward when put into the chamber. Some animals might attempt to climb up the sides. Unless the chamber is precharged, nonburrowing animals will initially be exposed to CO_2 at a lower concentration, and some might hyperventilate, struggle, and stagger (CCAC, 1980). The number of animals placed in a chamber at a given time depends on the size and temperament of the species, but the animals should not be crowded.

PHYSICAL METHODS

Physical methods of euthanasia include stunning, cervical dislocation, decapitation, gunshot, electrocution, decompression, use of a captive bolt, microwave irradiation, exsanguination, rapid freezing, and pithing. Physical methods are appropriate in three general situations: with easily handled small animals whose anatomic features are compatible with the method used; with large farm animals; and in situations in which other methods might invalidate the experimental results. Some people consider physical methods of euthanasia aesthetically displeasing or repulsive. However, some physical methods cause less fear and anxiety and can be more rapid, painless, humane, and practical than other forms of euthanasia. The skill and experience of the attendant are paramount when physical methods are used, because trauma is often involved. If they are not performed correctly, animals might be injured, have various degrees of consciousness, and suffer pain and distress. Some of the methods, particularly stunning and pithing, do not ensure death and therefore necessitate followup measures, such as exsanguination or decapitation. Before using physical methods, inexperienced persons should practice on carcasses or anesthetized animals that are scheduled for euthanasia until they are proficient in performing the methods properly and humanely.

Stunning

Stunning is used primarily on small laboratory animals with relatively thin craniums. A sharp blow must be delivered to the central skull bones with sufficient force to produce massive hemorrhage and thus immediate depression of the CNS. When it is done properly, unconsciousness is immediate. After stunning, the animal should be killed immediately by another procedure, such as exsanguination or decapitation.

Properly performed stunning is humane. However, the probability of improper stunning is rather high for inexperienced personnel. Stunning should be used only by properly trained persons and when other means are inappropriate or unavailable. Stunning can affect the release and the concentration of catecholamines and other neurotransmitters and perhaps other brain metabolites.

Captive-bolt guns are commonly used for stunning large farm animals. After stunning with a captive bolt, euthanasia must be performed by another means. A penetrating captive bolt has been described for euthanasia of dogs and rabbits (Dennis et al., 1988).

Cervical Dislocation

Cervical dislocation is commonly used to euthanatize small laboratory animals (e.g., poultry, mice, and immature rats and rabbits). It causes almost immediate loss of consciousness because of cerebral shock, and all voluntary motor and sensory functions cease because of damage to the spinal cord. This method can cause considerable involuntary muscle activity. However, there is no evidence that animals feel pain, if it is performed correctly. The technique consists of a separation of the skull and brain from the spinal cord by anteriorly directed pressure applied to the base of the skull.

Decapitation

Decapitation with a guillotine (or heavy shears) is used primarily when pharmacologic agents and CO_2 are contraindicated, e.g., in pharmacologic and biochemical studies. The procedure causes rapid death if properly performed. An animal should be properly restrained, and its head must be completely severed from its body at the atlanto-occipital joint. Decapitation is often aesthetically unpleasant and dangerous for the operator. The guillotine must be kept in good operating condition, and the blade must be sharp. The equipment should be thoroughly cleaned after each use.

Gunshot

Gunshot is an effective and practical means of humanely killing some animals in particular circumstances, such as field studies, rural settings (farm animals), and emergencies.

Microwave Irradiation

Euthanasia by microwave irradiation with focused beam instruments is used by neurobiologists to fix brain metabolites without losing the anatomic integrity of the brain. Unconsciousness and death occur in less than a second. Instruments are expensive, and only animals the size of mice or rats can be euthanatized with currently available equipment (AVMA, 1986). Standard kitchen microwave appliances are not appropriate, because their beams are diffuse and animals might experience severe pain or distress.

Double Pithing

Double pithing is an effective method of killing some poikilotherms (cold-blooded animals). A sharp needle with a diameter appropriate to the size of the animal is quickly inserted in a cranial direction through the foramen magnum and is rotated so as to crush the brain bilaterally. The needle is then inserted in a caudal direction at the same point of entry and rotated to destroy the spinal cord. Pithing requires dexterity and skill and should be conducted only by trained personnel.

Rapid Freezing

Rapid freezing is used by neurobiologists, because it instantaneously inactivates enzymes in the brain. Immersion of the entire animal in liquid nitrogen achieves rapid death of an animal that weighs less than 40 g. Heavier animals should be anesthetized before this technique is used. Suitable equipment and properly trained personnel are required.

Exsanguination

Because of the anxiety associated with extreme hypovolemia, exsanguination should be done only in sedated, stunned, or anesthetized animals (AVMA, 1986).

NONINHALATIONAL PHARMACOLOGIC AGENTS

Several noninhalational agents are used for euthanasia. Although death can be induced by administering these drugs by several routes, intravenous administration is preferred, because of its smooth induction, rapid action, and reliability. Intrapulmonic injection should be avoided. Intracardiac injection should be used discriminatingly, because it requires considerable skill; the injection might be painful, and, if the drug is accidentally discharged outside the heart, death will be slow and painful. Intracardiac injection of drugs is recommended only for moribund, anesthetized, or comatose animals. Intraperitoneal administration requires higher doses and leads to prolonged dying, and induction can be marked by ataxia and struggling.

Barbituric Acid Derivatives

The barbiturates are used extensively and are considered the agents of choice for most euthanasia on both aesthetic and scientific bases. Barbiturates are humane, safe, and efficient when properly administered. Intravenous administration of a barbiturate produces a smooth and rapid onset of unconsciousness without disturbing behavior before death. Sodium pentobarbital has been used as a standard against which other agents and methods for euthanasia are often compared. Other barbiturates are available, and overdoses of them will produce similar results. But none has any advantage over sodium pentobarbital, and most are considerably more expensive.

There are several disadvantages in the use of barbiturates. Animals must be handled individually. Because there is a potential for human drug abuse, barbiturates are controlled substances that require Drug Enforcement Agency registration and record-keeping. Trained personnel are required to administer the drugs intravenously. There can be aesthetically unpleasant behavior and some animal discomfort when the drugs are not administered intravenously.

For nervous and intractable animals, preinduction with tranquilizers or sedatives might be appropriate.

An overdose of barbiturates causes death by depression of vital medullary respiratory and vasomotor centers. Within seconds of intravenous administration, the animal simply relaxes, closes its eyes, and stops breathing. Cardiac arrest follows, but the heart can continue to beat for a few minutes. The effect depends on dose, concentration, and rate of injection.

Commercial preparations of sodium pentobarbital for euthanasia contain 260-390 mg/ml and are usually given intravenously at a dose of approximately 100 mg/kg of body weight.

T-61

T-61 is a nonbarbiturate, nonnarcotic euthanatizing agent. It was formerly used for euthanasia, but its commercial production was discontinued in Great Britain in 1962 and in the United States in 1989. T-61 can be used humanely with close adherence to the recommended rate of administration. It is included here because supplies of the agent exist and some still use it.

Other Drugs

Other injectable pharmacologic agents are available for restraint, immobilization, analgesia, and anesthesia of animals, such as ketamine hydrochloride, xylazine, and opioids. Although it might be possible to cause death with high doses of these drugs, they are not recommended for euthanasia, because such use would be impractical and might produce convulsions before death.

RECOMMENDATIONS FOR SPECIFIC ANIMALS

Table 7-2 lists recommendations for euthanasia of particular species.

TABLE 7-2 General Recommendations for Euthanasia (*Categorized by Species*)

Species	Agent or Method
Dogs and cats	Barbiturates Carbon dioxide[a] (small dogs)
Ferrets	Barbiturates
Rabbits	Barbiturates Stunning[b] Cervical dislocation (small rabbits) Carbon dioxide[a]
Rodents	Carbon dioxide[a] Barbiturates Cervical dislocation (< 200 g) Stunning[b] Decapitation
Nonhuman primates	Barbiturates
Birds	Carbon dioxide[a] Barbiturates Cervical dislocation Decapitation Stunning[b]
Snakes and lizards	Barbiturates or inhalant anesthetics Stunning[b]
Turtles, terrapins, and tortoises	Barbiturates or inhalant anesthetics Stunning[b]
Crocodilians	Barbiturates Gunshot
Frogs, toads, newts, and salamanders	Stunning[b] Anesthetic overdose Tricaine methanesultate (MS 222)
Fish	Stunning[b] Tricaine methanesultate (MS 222)

[a]Not suitable for newborn or newly hatched animals.
[b]Followed by immediate killing by another method.

DOGS AND CATS

Intravenous administration of sodium pentobarbital at 90-100 mg/kg, 3 times the anesthetic dose, should ensure respiratory and then cardiac arrest in dogs and cats. This is the procedure of choice for these species. Intracardiac injection can be used in anesthetized or moribund dogs and cats.

High concentrations (40-70%) of CO_2 can also be used.

FERRETS

Intraperitoneal administration of sodium pentobarbital (100-120 mg/kg) is a practical means of euthanatizing ferrets.

RABBITS

The preferable means of euthanatizing rabbits is intravenous injection of sodium pentobarbital (100 mg/kg). The intracardiac route should be used only in anesthetized or moribund animals.

Rabbits can also be killed by cranial concussion (stunning) or by cervical dislocation (recommended only for small rabbits). Extreme care should be used to ensure that these techniques are properly performed by trained personnel.

CO_2 at concentrations over 40% is safe and effective for euthanatizing rabbits.

LABORATORY RODENTS

CO_2 is considered acceptable for euthanatizing rodents. Newborn animals are more resistant to CO_2 than older animals.

Sodium pentobarbital (150-200 mg/kg) is also commonly used. Intraperitoneal administration is acceptable, because intravenous injection is difficult. Intracardiac and intrapulmonic administration are recommended only for anesthetized animals.

Cervical dislocation can be used to kill animals that weigh less than 250 g. Hamsters and guinea pigs are more difficult to kill with this method, because of their short necks, stronger neck muscles, and loose skin over the neck and shoulders.

Stunning by cervical concussion can cause unconsciousness, but extreme care should be used to ensure that this technique is performed properly. After stunning, the animal should be killed immediately by another procedure, such as exsanguination or decapitation.

Decapitation with a guillotine is recommended only when use of drugs is contraindicated. Successful decapitation, like cervical dislocation, is more difficult in hamsters and guinea pigs than in rats, because of the anatomy of their necks and shoulders.

NONHUMAN PRIMATES

Nonhuman primates are usually euthanatized by an intravenous overdose of sodium pentobarbital (100 mg/kg).

BIRDS

Euthanasia in a CO_2 chamber is effective for birds and is safe.

Sodium pentobarbital (100 mg/kg) can be administered intravenously or intraperitoneally.

Cervical dislocation of birds is rapid and inexpensive. It can be done manually with small birds. In large fowl, like turkeys and geese, an instrument like Burdizzo forceps is needed.

Decapitation with a guillotine or shears is effective with small birds.

Small birds can also be stunned (see guidelines on stunning).

AMPHIBIANS, FISH, AND REPTILES

Euthanasia of amphibians, fish, and reptiles has been studied less than euthanasia of other animals, and guidelines are less available.

When euthanasia of poikilothermic animals and aquatic animals is performed, the differences in their metabolism, respiration, and tolerance of cerebral hypoxia might preclude some procedures that would be acceptable in terrestrial mammals (AVMA, 1986).

Anatomic differences should also be considered. For example, veins can be hard to find. Some animals have a carapace. For physical methods, access to the CNS can be difficult, because the brain is relatively small and hard for inexperienced persons to find.

Euthanasia of Amphibians and Reptiles (UFAW/WSPA, 1989) suggests that, when physical methods of euthanasia of poikilothermic species are used, cooling to 4°C decreases metabolism and might facilitate handling; but there is no evidence that it raises the pain threshold. That report provides line drawings of the heads of various amphibians and reptiles with recommended locations for captive-bolt or firearm penetration.

Most amphibians, fishes, and reptiles can be euthanatized by cranial concussion followed by decapitation or some other physical method.

Decapitation with a guillotine or heavy shears is effective in some species that have appropriate anatomic features. It has previously been assumed that stopping blood supply to the brain by decapitation causes immediate unconsciousness followed by rapid loss of sensation. That view has recently been questioned, because the CNS of reptiles and amphibians tolerates hypoxic and hypotensive conditions (UFAW/WSPA, 1989). Decapitation should therefore be followed by pithing.

Pithing is an effective method of killing some poikilotherms, but death might not be immediate, unless both the brain and spinal cord are pithed, which is recommended. Pithing of only the spinal cord should be followed by decapitation or another appropriate procedure. The anatomic features of some species preclude this method. Pithing requires some dexterity and skill and should be conducted only by trained personnel.

Snakes and turtles have been killed by freezing after immobilization by cooling. However, the 1989 report of the Universities Federation for Animal Welfare and World Society for the Protection of Animals (UFAW/WSPA, 1989) does not recommend that method; formation of ice crystals on the skin and in tissues of an animal can cause pain or distress.

Sodium pentobarbital (60 mg/kg) or other barbiturates can be administered, depending on anatomic features, intravenously, intracardially, or into the abdominal or pleuroperitoneal cavity of most cold-blooded animals.

Tricaine methanesulfate (MS 222) can be administered by various routes to induce euthanasia. For aquatic animals, it can be placed in the water—an effective but expensive means of euthanasia that is not hazardous to personnel.

Snakes, lizards, turtles, frogs, and toads can be killed by overexposure to gaseous anesthetics, such as halothane or methoxyflurane, in a chamber or by mask. CO_2 can be used for terrestrial animals.

For additional reading on this subject, refer to *Amphibians: Guidelines for the Breeding, Care, and Management of Laboratory Animals* (NRC, 1974), *The Relief of Pain in Cold-Blooded Vertebrates* (Arena and Richardson, 1990), and *Anesthesia in Fish* (Brown, 1988).

References

Abelson, P. H. 1992. Diet and cancer in humans and rodents. Science 225:141. (Editorial)

Ader, R. 1967. The influence of psychological factors on disease susceptibility in animals. Pp. 219-238 in Husbandry of Laboratory Animals, M. L. Conalty, ed. London: Academic Press.

Allred, J. B., and G. G. Berntson. 1986. Is euthanasia of rats by decapitation inhumane? J. Nutr. 116:1859-1861.

Amyx, H. L. 1987. Control of animal pain and distress in antibody production and infectious disease studies. J. Am. Vet. Med. Assoc. 191(10):1287-1289.

Anand, K. J. S., D. Phil, and P. R. Hickey. 1987a. Pain and its effects in the human neonate and fetus. N. Eng. J. Med. 317(21):1321-1329.

Anand, K. J. S., W. G. Sippell, and A. Aynsley-Green. 1987b. Randomized trial of fentanyl anaesthesia in preterm babies undergoing surgery: Effects on the stress response. Lancet 1:243-248.

Antin, J., J. Gibbs, J. Holt, R. C. Young, and G. P. Smith. 1975. Cholecystokinin elicits the complete behavioral sequence of satiety in rats. J. Comp. Physiol. Psychol. 89:784-790.

Archer, J. 1970. Effects of population density on behaviour in rodents. Pp. 169-210 in Social Behaviour in Birds and Mammals, J. H. Crook, ed. New York: Academic Press.

Arena, P. C., and K. C. Richardson. 1990. The relief of pain in cold-blooded vertebrates. Australian Council for the Care of Animals in Research and Teaching (ACCART) News 3(1):1-4.

Arluke, A. 1990. Uneasiness among laboratory technicians. Lab Anim. 19(4):20-39.

AVMA (American Veterinary Medical Association). 1986. 1986 Report of the AVMA Panel on Euthanasia. J. Am. Vet. Med. Assoc. 188(3):252-268.

Bahga, H. S., and R. P. Link. 1966. Cardiovascular effects of two phenothiazines: Fluphenazine and trifluoperazine. Am. J. Vet. Res. 27:81.

Barclay, R. J., W. J. Herbert, and T. B. Poole. 1988. The Disturbance Index: A Behavioral Method for Assessing the Severity of Common Laboratory Procedures on Rodents. Hertfordshire, UK: Universities Federation for Animal Welfare. 35 pp.

117

Bayne, K., H. Mainzer, S. Dexter, G. Campbell, F. Yamada, and S. Suomi. 1991. The reduction of abnormal behaviors in individually housed rhesus monkeys (*Macaca mulatta*) with a foraging/grooming board. Am. J. Primatol. 23(1):23-35.

Beaver, B. V. 1989. Environmental enrichment for laboratory animals. ILAR News 31(2):5-13.

Benson, G. J., and J. C. Thurmon. 1979. Anesthesia of swine under field conditions. J. Am. Vet. Med. Assoc. 194:594.

Berlyne, D. E. 1960. Conflict, Arousal and Curiosity. New York: McGraw-Hill. 350 pp.

Berson, B., G. Bernston, E. Zipf, M. Torello, and W. Kirk. 1983. Vasopressin-induced antinociception: An investigation into its physiological and hormonal basis. Endocrinology 113:337-343.

Bertram, B. C. R. 1978. Living in groups: Predators and prey. Pp. 64-96 in Behavioural Ecology: An Evolutionary Approach, 1st ed., J. R. Krebs, and N. B. Davies, eds. Sunderland, Mass.: Sinauer.

Bloom, K. R., and M. Cook. 1989. Environmental enrichment: Behavioral responses of rhesus to puzzle feeders. Lab Anim. 18(4):25-31.

Bloomsmith, M. 1989. Feeding enrichment for captive great apes. Pp. 336-356 in Housing, Care and Psychological Well-Being of Captive and Laboratory Primates, E. F. Segal, ed. Park Ridge, N.J.: Noyes Publications.

Bloomstrand, M. 1987. An analysis of feeding enrichment for captive chimpanzees. Diss. Abstr. Int. 48(5-B):1545.

Boccia, M. L. 1989. Long-term effects of a natural foraging task on aggression and sterotypies in socially housed pigtail macaques. Lab. Primate Newsl. 28(2):18-19.

Bonner, W. B., M. E. Keeling, E. T. Van Ormer, and J. E. Haynie. 1972. Ketamine anesthesia in chimpanzees and other great ape species. The Chimpanzee 5:255-268.

Booij, L. H. D. J., R. P. Edwards, Y. J. Sohn, R. D. Miller. 1980. Comparative cardiovascular and neuromuscular effects of ORG NC45, pancuronium, metocurine and d-tubocurarine. Anesth. Anagl. (Cleveland) 19:26-30.

Booth, N. H., and L. E. McDonald, eds. 1982. Non-narcotic analgesics. Pp. 297-320 in Veterinary Pharmacology and Therapeutics, 5th ed. Ames: Iowa State University Press.

Bowd, A. D. 1980. Ethics and animal experimentation. Am. Psychol. 35:224-225.

Breazile, J. E. 1987. Physiologic basis and consequences of distress in animals. J. Am. Vet. Med. Assoc. 191(10):1212-1215.

Breese, C. E., and N. H. Dodman. 1984. Xylazine-ketamine-oxymorphone: An injectable anesthetic combination in swine. J. Am. Vet. Med. Assoc. 184:182-183.

Breland, K., and M. Breland. 1961. The misbehavior of organisms. Am. Psychol. 16:681-684.

Brown, L. A. 1988. Anesthesia in Fish. Vet. Clin. N. Am. 18(2):317-330.

Bustad, L. K. 1982. An educator's approach to euthanasia. Lab Anim. 11(4):37-41.

Calderwood, H. W., A. M. Klide, B. B. Cohn, and L. R. Soma. 1971. Cardiorespiratory effects of tiletamine in cats. Am. J. Vet. Res. 32(10):1511-1515.

Cannon, W. B. 1929. Bodily Changes in Pain, Hunger, Fear and Rage: An account of recent researches into the function of emotional excitement. New York: Appleton. 404 pp.

Cass, N. W., A. Brown, K. C. Ng, and D. G. Lampard. 1980. Dosage patterns of non-depolarizing neuromuscular blockers in the sheep. Anaesth. Intens. Care 8:13-15.

CCAC (Canadian Council on Animal Care). 1980. Guide to the Care and Use of Experimental Animals. Vol. 1. Ontario, Canada: Canadian Council on Animal Care. 120 pp.

CFR (Code of Federal Regulations), Title 9 (Animals and Animal Products), Subchapter A (Animal Welfare), Parts 1-3. Copies available from: Animal Care Staff, Regulatory Enforcement and Animal Care, APHIS, USDA, Federal Building, Room 268, Hyattsville, MD 20782.

Chamove, A. S., and J. R. Anderson. 1988. Impact of feeding practices on growth and behavior of stump-tailed macaques (*Macaca arctoides*). Bull. Soc. Herpetol. France 11:231-246.

Chamove, A. S., J. G. Anderson, S. C. Morgan-Jones, and S. P. Jones. 1982. Deep woodchip litter: Hygiene, feeding, and behavioral enhancement in eight primate species. Int. J. Study Anim. Prob. 3:308-318.

Chen, G. 1973. Sympathomimetic anesthetics. Can. Anaesth. Soc. J. 20(2):180-185.

Clarke, K. W., and L. W. Hall. 1969. "Xylazine"—A new sedative for horses and cattle. Vet. Rec. 8:512-517.

Clifford, D. H. 1957. Effect of preanesthetic medication with chlorpromazine, meperidine and promazine on pentobarbital anesthesia in the cat. J. Am. Vet. Med. Assoc. 156:415-418.

Clifford, D. H. 1984. Preanesthesia, anesthesia, analgesia and euthanasia. Pp. 527-562 in Lab. Anim. Med., J. G. Fox, B. J. Cohen, and F. M. Loew, eds. Orlando, Fla.: Academic Press.

Collette, W. L., and W. F. Meriwether. 1965. Some changes in the peripheral blood of dogs after administration of certain tranquilizers and narcotics. Vet. Med./Small Anim. Clinic 60:1223.

Conahan, S. T., and W. H. Vogel. 1986. The effect of diazepam administration on heart rate and mean arterial blood pressure in resting and stressed conscious rats. Res. Commun. Chem. Pathol. Pharmacol. 53(3):301-317.

Connolly, R., and F. W. Quimby. 1978. Acepromazine-ketamine anesthesia in the rhesus monkey (*Macaca mulatta*). Lab. Anim. Sci. 28:72-74.

Cooper, B. Y., and C. J. Vierck, Jr. 1986. Vocalizations as measures of pain in monkeys. Pain 26(3):393-407.

Copland, V. S., S. C. Haskins, and J. D. Patz. 1987. Oxymorphone: Cardiovascular, pulmonary, and behavioral effects in dogs. Am. J. Vet. Med. Res. 48(11):1626-1630.

Covino, B. G., H. A. Fozzard, K. Rehder, eds. 1985. Effects of Anesthesia: Clinical Physiology Series. Bethesda, Md.: American Physiological Society. 224 pp.

Crane, S. W. 1987. Perioperative analgesia: A surgeon's perspective. J. Am. Vet. Med. Assoc. 191:1254-1257.

Cronin, G. M., P. R. Wiepkema, and J. M. van Ree. 1986. Endorphins implicated in stereotypies on tethered sows. Experientia 42(2):198-199.

Cullen, L. K., and R. S. Jones. 1977. Clinical observations on xylazine-ketamine anaesthesia in the cat. Vet. Rec. 101:115-116.

Curl, J. L., and L. L. Peters. 1983. Ketamine hydrochloride and xylazine hydrochloride anaesthesia in the golden hamster (*Mesocricetus auratus*). Lab. Anim. 17:290-293.

Dahlstrom, B. E., L. K. Paalzow, C. Lindberg, and C. Bogentoft. 1979. Pharmacokinetics and analgesic effect of pethidine (meperidine) and its metabolites in the rat. Drug Metab. Dispos. 7(2):108-112.

Daly, M. 1973. Early stimulation of rodents: A critical review of present interpretations. Br. J. Psy. 64:435-460.

Dantzer, R. 1986. Behavioral, physiological and functional aspects of stereotyped behavior: A review and re-interpretation. J. Anim. Sci. 62(6):1776-1786.

Dawkins, M. S. 1976. Towards an objective method of assessing welfare in domestic fowl. Appl. Anim. Ethol. 2(3):245-254.

Dawkins, M. S. 1983. Battery hens name their price: Consumer demand theory and the measurement of ethological "needs". Anim. Behav. 31:1195-1205.

Dawkins, M. S. 1990. From an animal's point of view: Motivation, fitness and animal welfare. Behav. Brain Sci. 13:1-61.

Denenberg, V. 1969. The Effects of early experience. Pp. 95-130 in Behaviour of Domestic Animals, E. S. E. Hafez, ed. Baltimore, Md.: Williams & Wilkins.

Dennis, M. B. Jr., W. K. Dong, K. A. Weisbrod, and C. A. Elchlepp. 1988. Use of captive bolt as a method of euthanasia in larger laboratory animal species. Lab. Anim. Sci. 38(4):459-462.

Denny, H. R., and J. N. Lucke. 1977. Anaesthetic and surgical technique for bilateral adrenalectomy in stress sensitive pigs. Res. Vet. Sci. 23:372-377.

DiGregorio, G. 1990. The effects of woodchips and buried food on behavior patterns and psychological well-being of captive rhesus monkeys. Diss. Abstr. Int. 50(12B):5924.

Dodman, N. H., L. Shuster, M. H. Court, and R. Dixon. 1987. Investigation into the use of narcotic antagonists in the treatment of a stereotypical behavior pattern (crib biting) in the horse. Am. J. Vet. Res. 48(2):311-319.

Dodman, N. H., G. H. Clark, M. H. Court, L. L. Fikes, and R. J. Boudrieau. 1992. Epidural opioid administration for postoperative pain relief in the dog. pp. 274-277 in Animal Pain, C. E. Short and A. Van Poznak, eds. New York: Churchill Livingstone, Inc.

Draisci, G., and M. J. Iadarola. 1989. Temporal analysis of increases in C-fos, preprodynorphin and preproenkephalin mRNAs in rat spinal cord. Brain Res. 6(1):31-37.

Dresser, R. 1988. Assessing harm and justification in animal research: Federal policy opens the laboratory door. Rutgers Law Rev. 40(3):723-795.

Dubner, R. 1985. Specialization in nociceptive pathways: Sensory discrimination, sensory modulation and neural connectivity. Pp. 111-137 in Advances in Pain Research and Therapy, vol. 9, H. L. Fields, R. Dubner, and F. Cervero, eds. New York: Raven Press.

Dubner, R. 1987. Research on pain mechanisms in animals. J. Am. Vet. Med. Assoc. 191(10):1273-1276.

Dubner, R., and G. J. Bennett. 1983. Spinal and trigeminal mechanisms of nociception. Ann. Rev. Neurosci. 6:381-418.

Dubner, R., B. Sessle, and A. T. Storey. 1978. The Neural Basis of Oral and Facial Function. New York: Plenum Press. 483 pp.

Dubner, R., D. R. Kenshalo, Jr., W. Maixner, M. C. Bushnell, and J. L. Oliveras. 1989. The correlation of monkey medullary dorsal horn neuronal activity and the perceived intensity of noxious heat stimuli. J. Neurophysiol. 62(2):450-457.

Durant, N. N., M. C. Houwertjes, J. F. Crul. 1980. Comparison of the neuromuscular blocking properties of ORG NC45 and pancuronium in the rat, cat and rhesus monkey. Br. J. Anaesth. 52:723-730.

Durant, N. N., I. G. Marshall, D. S. Savage. 1979. The neuromuscular and autonomic blocking activities of pancuronium analogues, in the cat. J. Pharm. Pharmacol. 31:831-836.

Eberhardson B., G. Olsson, L. E. Appelgren, and S. O. Jacobson. 1979. Pharmacokinetic studies of phenylbutazone in cattle. J. Vet. Pharmacol. Ther. 2:31-37.

Eger, E. I. 1978. MAC. Pp. 1-25 in Anesthetic Uptake and Action, E. E. I. Eger, ed. Baltimore, Md.: Williams & Wilkins.

Eger, E. I. II, L. J. Saidman, and B. Brandstater. 1965. Minimum alveolar anesthetic concentration: A standard of anesthetic potency. Anesthesiology 26:756-763.

Eisemann, C. H., W. K. Jorgenson, D. J. Merritt, M. J. Rice, B. W. Cribb, P. D. Webb, and M. P. Zalucki. 1984. Do insects feel pain?—A biological review. Experientia 40:164-167.

Fajzi, K., V. Reinhardt, and M. D. Smith. 1989. A review of environmental enrichment strategies for singly caged nonhuman primates. Lab. Anim. 18(2):23-35.

Fentress, J. C. 1973. Specific and nonspecific factors in the causation of behavior. Pp. 155-224 in Perspectives in Ethology, vol. 1, P. P. G. Bateson and P. H. Klopfer, eds. New York: Plenum Press.

Field, W. E., J. Yelnosky, J. Mundy, and J. Mitchell. 1966. Use of droperidol and fentanyl for analgesia and sedation in primates. J. Am. Vet. Med. Assoc. 149(7):896-901.

Finley, R. S. 1990. Pain management with spinally administered opioids. Am. J. Hosp. Pharm. 47:S14-S17.

Fiorito, G. 1986. Is there pain in invertebrates? Behav. Processes 12:383-388.

Flecknell, P. A. 1984. The relief of pain in laboratory animals. Lab. Anim. 18(2):147-160.

Flecknell, P. A. 1985. Recognition and alleviation of pain in animals. Pp. 61-77 in Advances in Animal Welfare Science. Boston, Mass.: Martinus Nijholt.

Flecknell, P. A. 1987. Laboratory Animal Anesthesia. London: Academic Press. 156 pp.

Flecknell, P. A., J. H. Liles, and R. Wootton. 1989. Reversal of fentanyl/fluanisone neuroleptanalgesia in the rabbit using mixed agonist/antagonist opioids. Lab. Anim. 23:147-155.

Gantt, W. H., J. E. O. Newton, F. L. Royer, and J. H. Stephens. 1966. Effect of person. Cond.
Reflex 1:18-35.

Gärtner, K., C. Büttner, K. Döhler, R. Friedel, J. Lindena, and I. Trautschold. 1980. Stress
response of rat to handling and experimental procedures. Lab. Anim. (England) 14:267-
274.

Gilman, A. G., T. W. Rall, A. S. Nies, and P. Taylor. 1990. Goodman and Gilman's The
Pharmacological Basis of Therapeutics, 8th ed. New York: Pergamon Press. 1811 pp.

Gleed, R. D. 1987. Tranquilizers and sedatives. Pp. 16-27 in Principles and Practice of Veterinary Anesthesia, C. E. Short, ed. Baltimore, Md.: Williams & Wilkins.

Goldstein, D. 1987. Stress-induced activation of the sympathetic nervous system. Bailliere's
Clin. Endocrinol. Metab. 1:253-278.

Gracely, R. H., P. McGrath, and R. Dubner. 1978. Ratio scales of sensory and affective verbal
pain descriptors. Pain 5:5-18.

Graham-Jones, O. 1960. Tranquilizer and paralytic drugs: An international survey of animal
restraint techniques. Int. Zoo Yearb. 2:300.

Graham-Jones, O. 1964. Restraint and anesthesia of some captive wild mammals. Vet. Rec.
76:1216.

Green, C. J. 1975. Neuroleptanalgesic drug combinations in the anaesthetic management of
small laboratory animals. Lab. Anim. 9:161-178.

Green, C. J. 1978. The prevention of apprehension and pain in experimental animals. Pp. 116-
124 in The Reduction and Prevention of Suffering in Animal Experiments. Proceedings of
the Royal Society for the Prevention of Cruelty to Animals Symposium. London.

Green, C. J., J. Knight, S. Precious, and S. Simpkin. 1981a. Metomidate, etomidate, and
fentanyl as injectable anaesthetic agents in mice. Lab. Anim. 15:171-175.

Green, C. J., J. Knight, S. Precious, and S. Simpkin. 1981b. Ketamine alone and combined
with diazepam or xylazine in laboratory animals: A 10 year experience. Lab. Anim.
15:163-170.

Greenstein, E. T. 1975. Ketamine HCl, a dissociative anesthetic for squirrel monkeys (*Saimiri
sciureus*). Lab. Anim. Sci. 25(6):774-777.

Gregg, R. 1989. Spinal analgesia. Anesthesiology Clinics N. Am. 7:79-100.

Hansen, B., E. Hardie, and M. Young. 1990. Recognition of acute pain and distress in the dog.
Humane Innovations and Alternatives in Animal Experimentation 4:170-172.

Hardie E. M, G. E. Hardee, and C. A. Rawlings. 1985. Pharmacokinetics of flunixin meglumine in dogs. Am. J. Vet. Res. 46(1):235-237.

Hardy, J. D., H. G. Wolff, and H. Goodell. 1952. Pain Sensation and Reactions. Baltimore,
Md.: Williams & Wilkins. 435 pp.

Hargreaves, K. M., and R. Dubner. 1991. Mechanisms of pain and analgesia. In Management
of Pain and Anxiety in Dental Practice, R. Dionne and J. Phero, eds. New York: Elsevier.
In press.

Hargreaves, K., R. Dionne, and G. Mueller. 1983. Plasma beta endorphin-like immunoreactivity, pain and anxiety following administration of placebo in oral surgery patients. J. Dent.
Res. 62:1170-1173.

Hargreaves, K. M., G. P. Mueller, R. Dubner, D. Goldstein, and R. A. Dionne. 1987. Corticotropin-releasing factor (CRF) produces analgesia in humans and rats. Brain Res. 422(1):154-
157.

Hargrove, J. C., J. E. Heavner, R. D. Guthrie, and W. R. Morton. 1980. Age dependent
ketamine pharmacodynamics in the pigtail monkey (*Macaca nemestrina*). Proc. West.
Pharmacol. Soc. 23:129-133.

Harkness, J. E., and J. E. Wagner. 1983. The Biology and Medicine of Rabbit and Rodents,
2nd ed. Philadelphia, Pa.: Lea and Febiger. 55 pp.

Hartsfield, S. M. 1987. Machines and breathing systems for administration of inhalation anesthetics. Pp. 395-418 in Principles and Practice of Veterinary Anesthesia, C. E. Short, ed. Baltimore, Md.: Williams & Wilkins.

Harvey, R. C. and J. Walberg. 1987. Special considerations for anesthesia and analgesia in research animals. Pp. 380-392 in Principles and Practice of Veterinary Anesthesia, C. E. Short, ed. Baltimore, Md.: Williams & Wilkins.

Heavner, J. E. 1970. Morphine for postsurgical use in cats. J. Am. Vet. Med. Assoc. 156:1018.

Hediger, H. 1955. Studies on the Psychology and Behaviour of Captive Animals in Zoos and Circuses. London: Butterworths Scientific Publications.

Hellyer, P., W. W. Muir, J. A. E. Hubbell, and J. Sally. 1988. Cardiorespiratory effects of the intravenous administration of tiletamine-zolazepam to cats. Vet. Surg. 17(2):105-110.

Hennessy, J. W., and S. Levine. 1979. Stress, arousal, and the pituitary-adrenal system: A psychoendocrine hypothesis. Pp. 134-178 in Progress in Psychobiology, J. M. Sprague and A. N. Epstein, eds. New York: Academic Press.

Higgins, A. J. 1985. The biology, pathophysiology and control of eicosanoids in inflammation. J. Vet. Pharmacol. Ther. 8(1):1-18.

Hildebrand, S. V., and G. A. Howitt. 1984. Dosage requirement of pancuronium in halothane-anesthetized ponies: A comparison of cumulative and single-dose administration. Am. J. Vet. Res. 45:2441-2444.

Hobbs, B. A., T. G. Rolhall, T. L. Sprenkel, and K. L. Anthony. 1991. Comparison of several combinations for anesthesia in rabbits. Am. J. Vet. Res. 5:669-674.

Hofer, M. A. 1978. Hidden regulatory processes in early social relationships. Pp. 135-166 in Perspectives in Ethology: Social Behavior, vol. 3, P. P. G. Bateson and P. H. Klopfer, eds. New York: Plenum Press.

Hoffman, P. E. 1974. Clinical evaluation of xylazine as a chemical restraining agent, sedative, and analgesic in horses. J. Am. Vet. Med. Assoc. 164(1):42-45.

Holzgrefe, H. H., J. M. Everitt, and E. M. Wright. 1987. Alpha-chloralose as a canine anesthetic. Lab. Anim. Sci. 37(5):587-595.

Hopkins, T. J. 1972. Clinical pharmacology of xylazine in cattle. Austral. Vet. J. 48:109-112.

Hosobuchi, Y., J. E. Adams, and R. Linchitz. 1977. Pain relief by electrical stimulation of the central gray matter in humans and its reversal by naloxone. Science 197:183-186.

Houdeshell J. W, and P. W. Hennessey. 1977. A new nonsteroidal, anti-inflammatory analgesic for horses. J. Equine Med. Surg. 1:57-63.

Hughes, B. O., and I. W. H. Duncan. 1988. The notion of ethological "need", models of animal motivation and animal welfare. Anim. Behav. 36:1696-1707.

Hughes, H. C. 1981. Anesthesia of laboratory animals. Lab. Anim. 10:40-56.

Hughes, H. C., W. J. White, and C. M. Lang. 1975. Guidelines for the use of tranquilizers, anesthetics, and analgesics in laboratory animals. Vet. Anesth. 2:19-24.

Hughes, H. C., and C. M. Lang. 1983. Control of pain in dogs and cats. Pp. 207-216 in Animal Pain: Perception and Alleviation, R. L. Kitchell, H. H. Erickson, eds. Bethesda, Md.: American Physiological Society.

Hughes, R., and D. J. Chapple. 1976. Effects of non-depolarizing neuromuscular blocking agents on peripheral autonomic mechanisms in cats. Br. J. Anaesth. 48:59-68.

Hylden, J. L., F. Anton, and R. L. Nahin. 1989. Spinal lamina I projection neurons in the rat: Collateral innervation of parabrachial area and thalamus. Neuroscience 28(1):27-37.

Iadarola, M. J., L. S. Brady, G. Draisci, and R. Dubner. 1988. Enhancement of dynorphin gene expression in spinal cord following experimental inflammation: Stimulus specificity, behavioral parameters and opioid receptor binding. Pain 35(3):313-326.

IRAC (Interagency Research Animal Committee). 1985. U.S. Government Principles for Utilization and Care of Vertebrate Animals Used in Testing, Research, and Training. 1985. Prepared by the Interagency Research Animal Committee, National Institutes of Health

(Lead). Pp 81-83 in Guide for the Care and Use of Laboratory Animals. NIH Publication No. 85-23. Washington, D.C.: U. S. Department of Health and Human Services.

Jenkins, W. L. 1987. Pharmacologic aspects of analgesic drugs in animals: An overview. J. Am Vet. Assoc. 191(10):1231-1240.

Jones, J. B., and M. L. Simmons. 1968. Innovar-Vet.® as an intramuscular anesthetic for rats. Lab. Anim. Care 18(6):642-643.

Joris, J., R. Dubner, and K. Hargreaves. 1987. Opioid analgesia at peripheral sites: A target for opioids released during stress and inflammation? Anesth. Analg. 66:1277-1281.

Kaka, J. S., P. A. Klavano, and W. L. Hayton. 1979. Pharmacokinetics of ketamine in the horse. Am. J. Vet. Res. 40(7):978-981.

Kalpravidh, M., W. V. Lumb, M. Wright, and R. B. Heath. 1984. Analgesic effects of butorphanol in horses: Dose-response studies. Am. J. Vet. Res. 45(2):211-216.

Kamerling, S. G., W. M. Cravens, and C. A. Bagwell. 1988. Objective assessment of detomidine-induced analgesia and sedation in the horse. Eur. J. Pharm. 151(1):1-8.

Kenshalo, D. R., Jr., E. H. Chudler, F. Anton, and R. Dubner. 1988. SI nociceptive neurons participate in the encoding process by which monkeys perceive the intensity of noxious thermal stimulation. Brain Res. 454(1-2):378-382.

Kisloff, B. 1975. Ketamine-paraldehyde anesthesia for rabbits. Am. J. Vet. Res. 36(7):1033-1034.

Kitchell, R. L., H. H. Erickson, E. Carstens, and L. E. Davis, eds. 1983. Animal Pain: Perception and Alleviation. Bethesda, Md.: American Physiological Society. 221 pp.

Kitchell, R. L., and R. D. Johnson. 1985. Assessment of Pain in Animals. Pp. 113-140 in Animal Stress, G. P. Moberg, ed. Bethesda, Md.: American Physiological Society.

Kitchen, H., A. Aronson, J. L. Bittle, C. W. McPherson, D. B. Morton, S. P. Pakes, B. Rollin, A. N. Rowan, J. A. Sechzer, J. E. Vanderlip, J. A. Will, A. S. Clark, and J. S. Gloyd. 1987. Panel report of the colloquium on recognition and alleviation of animal pain and distress. J. Am. Vet. Med. Assoc. 191(10):1186-1191.

Klein, L. 1987. Neuromuscular Blocking Agents. Pp. 134-153 in Principles and Practice of Veterinary Anesthesia, C. E. Short, ed. Baltimore, Md.: Williams & Wilkins.

Klein, L., and C. Baetjer. 1974. Preliminary report: Xylazine and morphine sedation in the horse. Vet. Anesth. 2:2-4.

Klein, L., J. Hopkins, and H. Rosenberg. 1983. Different relationship of train-of-four to twitch and tetanus for vecuronium, pancuronium and gallamine. Anesthesiology. 59:A275.

Klein, L., T. Sylvina, and E. Beck. 1985. Neuromuscular blockade with d-tubocurarine, pancuronium and vecuronium in halothane anesthetized sheep. Proc. 2nd Intl. Cong. Vet. Anes. Oct:174 (abstract).

Klemm, W. R. 1976. Use of the immobility reflex ("animal hypnosis") in neuropharmacological studies. Pharmacol. Biochem. Behav. 4:85-94.

Klide, A. M. 1989. An hypothesis for the prolonged effect of acupuncture. Acupuncture Electrother. Res. 14(2):141-147.

Klide, A. M., and B. B. Martin. 1989. Methods of stimulating acupuncture points for treatment of chronic back pain in horses. J. Am. Vet. Med. Assoc. 195:1375-1379.

Klide, A. M., H. W. Calderwood, and L. R. Soma. 1975. Cardiopulmonary effects of xylazine in dogs. Am. J. Vet. Res. 36(7):931-935.

Kohn, C. W., and W. W. Muir. 1988. Selected aspects of the clinical pharmacology of visceral analgesics and gut motility modifying drugs in the horse. J. Vet. Intern. Med. 2(2):85-91.

Kolata, R. J., and C. A Rawlings. 1982. Cardiopulmonary effects of intravenous xylazine, ketamine, and atropine in the dog. Am. J. Vet. Res. 43(12):2196-2198.

Kruckenburg, S. M. 1979. Drugs and dosages. Appendix 2 in The Laboratory Rat, vols. 1 and 2, H. J. Baker, J. R. Lindsey, and S. H. Weisbroth, eds. London: Academic Press.

Landi, M., J. W. Krieder, C. M. Lang and L. P. Bullock. 1982. Effects of shipping on the immune function of mice. Am. J. Vet. Res. 43:1654-1657.

Latané, B., and D. Hothersall. 1972. Social attraction in animals. Pp. 259-275 in New Horizons in Psychology 2, P. C. Dodwell, ed. London: Penguin Books.

Leash, A. M., R. D. Beyer, and R. G. Wilber. 1973. Self-mutilation following Innovar-Vet.® injection in the guinea pig. Lab. Anim. Sci. 23:720-721.

Lefebvre, L., and G. Carli. 1985. Parturition in non-human primates: Pain and auditory concealment. Pain 21(4):315-327.

Levine, S. A. 1985. A definition of stress? Pp. 51-70 in Animal Stress, G. Moberg, ed. Bethesda, Md.: American Physiological Society.

Lewis, G. E., Jr., and P. J. Jennings, Jr. 1972. Effective sedation of laboratory animals using Innovar-Vet.® Lab. Anim. Sci. 22:430-432.

Lin, H. C., J. C. Thurmon, G. J. Benson, W. J. Tranquilli, and W. A. Olson. 1989. The hemodynamic response of calves to tiletamine-zolazepam anesthesia. Vet. Surg. 18(4):328-334.

Lindberg, D., and A. Smith. 1988. Organoleptic factors in animal feeding. Zoonooz. 61(12):14-15.

Line, S. W. 1987. Environmental enrichment for laboratory primates. J. Am. Vet. Med. Assoc. 190(7):854-859.

Line, S. W., and P. Houghton. 1987. Influence in an environmental enrichment device on general behavior and appetite in rhesus macaques. Lab. Anim. Sci. 37(4):508.

Lowe, J. E. 1969. Pentazocine (Talwin-V) for the relief of abdominal pain in ponies—A comparative evaluation with description of a colic model for analgesia evaluation. Proc. Am. Assoc. Equine Prac. Proc. Dec:31-46.

Ludders, J. W. 1992. Pharmacokinetics and the use of animals in research. Pp. 318-322 in Animal Pain, C. E. Short, A. Van Poznak, eds. New York: Churchill Livingstone.

Lumb, W. V. 1974. Euthanasia by noninhalant pharmacologic agents. J. Am. Vet. Med. Assoc. 165:851-852.

Lumb, W. V., and E. W. Jones. 1984. Veterinary Anesthesia. Philadelphia: Lea & Febiger. 693 pp.

Lumb, W. V., and A. F. Moreland. 1982. Chemical methods for euthanasia. Lab Anim. 11(4):29-35.

Maki, S., P. L. Alford, M. A. Bloomsmith, and J. Franklin. 1989. Food puzzle device simulating termite fishing for captive chimpanzees (Pan troglodytes). Am. J. Primatol. 1:71-78.

Malis, J. L. 1973. Analgesic testing in primates. Pp. 206-209 in Agonist and Antagonist Actions of Narcotic Analgesic Drugs, H. W. Kosterlitz, H. O. J. Collier, and J. E. Villarreal, eds. Baltimore, Md.: University Park Press.

Manley S. V., E. P. Steffey, G. A. Howitt, and M. Woliner. 1983. Cardiovascular and neuromuscular effects of pancuronium bromide in the pony. Am. J. Vet. Res. 44:1349-1353.

Markowitz, H. 1978. Engineering environments for behavioral opportunities in the zoo. Behav. Anal. Spring:34-47.

Markowitz, H. 1982. Behavioral Enrichment in the Zoo. New York: Van Nostrand Reinhold.

Marsboom, R., J. Mortelmans, J. Vercruysse, and D. Thienpont. 1962. Effect of sedation in gorillas and chimpanzees. Nord. Vet. Med. 14(1):95-101.

Marsboom, R., J. Mortelmans, and J. Vercruysse. 1963. Neuroleptanalgesia in monkeys. Vet. Rec. 75:132-133.

Martin, W. R. 1984. Pharmacology of opioids. Pharmacol. Rev. 35(4):283-323.

Mason, W. A. 1965. Determinants of social behavior in young chimpanzees. Pp. 335-364 in Behavior of Nonhuman Primates, Vol. 2, A. M. Schrier, H. F. Harlow, and F. Stollnitz, eds. New York: Academic Press.

Mason, W. A. 1967. Motivational aspects of social responsiveness in young chimpanzees. Pp. 103-126 in Early Behavior: Comparative and Developmental Approaches, H. W. Stevenson, E. H. Hess, and H. Rheingold, eds. New York: John Wiley & Sons, Inc.

Mason, W. A., and J. P. Capitanio. 1988. Formation and expression of filial attachment in rhesus monkeys raised with living and with inanimate mother substitutes. Dev. Psychol. 21(5):401-430.

Mayer, D. J., and D. D. Price. 1976. Central nervous systems of analgesia. Pain 2:379-404.

Mayer, D. J., T. W. Wolfle, H. Akil, B. Carder, and J. Liebeskind. 1971. Analgesia from electrical stimulation in the brainstem of the rat. Science 174:1351-1354.

Mazue, G., P. Richez, and J. Berthe. 1982. Pharmacology and comparative toxicology of nonsteroidal anti-inflammatory agents. Pp. 321-331 in Veterinary Pharmacology and Toxicology, Y. Ruckenbusch, P. L. Toutain, and G. D. Koritz, eds. Boston, Mass.: MTP.

McCormick, M. J., and M. A. Ashworth. 1971. Acepromazine and methoxyflurane anesthesia of immature New Zealand White Rabbits. Lab. Anim. Sci. 21(2):220-223.

Medway, Lord. 1980. Report of the Panel of Enquiry into Shooting and Angling. c/o Causeway, Horsham, Sussex, RH12 1HG, England.

Melzack, R., and P. D. Wall. 1965. Pain mechanisms: A new theory. Science 150:971-979.

Melzack, R., and T. H. Scott, 1957. The effects of early experience on the response to pain. J. Comp. Physiol. Psychol. 50:155-161.

Mendoza, S. P., and W. A. Mason. 1986. Contrasting responses to intruders and to involuntary separation by monogamous and polygynous New World monkeys. Physiol. Behav. 38(6):795-801.

Merin, R. G. 1975. Effect of anesthetics on the heart. Surg. Clin. N. Am. 55(4):759-774.

Mersky, H. 1979. Pain terms: A list with definitions and notes on usage. Pain 6:249-250.

Meyer, R. A., J. N. Campbell, and S. N. Raja. 1985. Peripheral neural mechanisms of cutaneous hyperalgesia. Pp. 53-71 in Advances in Pain Research and Therapy, H. L. Fields, R. Dubner, and F. Cervero, eds. New York: Raven Press.

Meyer-Holzapfel, M. 1968. Abnormal behavior in zoo animals. Pp. 476-503 in Abnormal Behavior in Animals, M. W. Fox, ed. Philadelphia: W. B. Saunders Co.

Mikeska, J. A., and W. R. Klemm. 1975. EEG evaluation of humaneness of asphyxia and decapitation euthanasia of the laboratory rat. Lab. Anim. Sci. 25(2):175-179.

Miller, N. E. 1956. Effects of drugs on motivation: The value of using a variety of measures. Ann. N. Y. Acad. Sci. 65:318-333.

Miller, R. D., ed. 1990. Anesthesia, 3rd ed. New York: Churchill Livingston. 115 pp.

Moazed, T. C., and A. V. Wolff. 1988. The raisin board as an environmental enrichment tool for laboratory primates. Lab. Primate Newsl. 27(1):16.

Moberg, G. P. 1987. Problems in defining stress and distress in animals. J. Am. Vet. Med. Assoc. 191(10):1207-1211.

Montgomery, C. A. 1987. Control of animal pain and distress in cancer and toxicologic research. J. Am. Vet. Med. Assoc. 191(10):1277-1281.

Moore, P. K. 1985. Pharmacology, Physiology and Clinical Relevance. New York: Cambridge University Press.

Morgan, R. J., L. B. Eddy, T. N. Solie, and C. C. Turbes. 1981. Ketamine-acepromazine as an anesthetic agent for chinchillas (*Chinchilla laniger*). Lab Anim. 15:281-283.

Morris, D. 1964. The response of animals to a restricted environment. Symp. Zool. Soc. Lond. 13:99-118.

Morton, D. B., and P. H. M. Griffiths. 1985. Guidelines on the recognition of pain, distress and discomfort in experimental animals and an hypothesis for assessment. Vet. Rec. 116:431-436.

Movshon, J. A. (Chairman). 1988. Anesthesia and paralysis in experimental animals: Report of a workshop held in Bethesda, Maryland, on October 27th, 1984. Visual Neurosci. 1:421-426.

Moye, R. J., A. Pailet, and M. W. Smith. 1973. Clinical use of xylazine in dogs and cats. Vet./ Small Anim. Clin. 63:236-241.

Muir, W. W., R. T. Skarda, and W. C. Sheehan. 1979. Hemodynamic and respiratory effects of xylazine-morphine sulfate in horses. Am. J. Vet. Res. 40(10):1417-1420.

Muir, W. W., R. A. Sams, R. H. Huffman, and J. S. Noonan. 1982. Pharmacodynamic and pharmacokinetic properties of diazepam in horses. Am. J. Vet. Res. 43(10):1756-1761.

Muir, W. W., J. A. E. Hubbell, and R. Skarda. 1989. Handbook of Veterinary Anesthesia. St. Louis, Mo.: C.V. Mosby. 340 pp.

Nahin, R. L., J. L. Hylden, M. J. Iadarola, and R. Dubner. 1989. Peripheral inflammation is associated with increased dynorphin immunoreactivity in both projection and local circuit neurons in the superficial dorsal horn of the rat lumbar spinal cord. Neurosci. Ltrs. 96(3):247-252.

Newton, G., and S. Levine, eds. 1968. Early Experience and Behavior. Springfield: C. C. Thomas. 785 pp.

Nilsson, E., and P. Janssen. 1961. Neurolept analgesia: An alternative to general anesthesia. Acta Anaesth. Scand. 5:73-78.

Novak, M. A., and S. J. Suomi. 1988. Psychological well-being of primates in captivity. Am. Psychol. 43(10):765-773.

NRC (National Research Council). 1974. Amphibians: Guidelines for the breeding, care, and management of laboratory animals. A report of the Institute of Laboratory Animal Resources Subcommittee on Amphibian Standards, National Research Council, National Academy of Sciences. Washington, D.C.: National Academy Press. 153 pp.

NRC (National Research Council). 1985. Guide for the Care and Use of Laboratory Animals. A report of the Institute of Laboratory Animal Resources Committee on Care and Use of Laboratory Animals. NIH Pub. No. 86-23. Washington, D.C.: U.S. Department of Health and Human Services. 83 pp.

NRC (National Research Council). 1990. Education and Training in the Care and Use of Laboratory Animals: A Guide for Developing Institutional Programs. A report of the Institute of Laboratory Animal Resources Committee on Educational Programs in Laboratory Animal Science, National Research Council, National Academy of Sciences. Washington, D. C.: National Academy Press. 139 pp.

NYAS (New York Academy of Sciences). 1988. Interdisciplinary Principles and Guidelines for the Use of Animals in Research, Testing, and Education. A report of the Ad Hoc Committee on Animal Research. New York: New York Academy of Sciences. 26 pp.

Oliveras, J. L., W. Maixner, R. Dubner, M. C. Bushnell, D. R. Kenshalo, Jr., G. H. Duncan, D. A. Thomas, and R. Bates. 1986. The medullary dorsal horn: A target for the expression of opiate effects on the perceived intensity of noxious heat. J. Neurosci. 6(10):3086-3093.

Orsini, J. A. 1988. Butorphanol tartrate. Pharmacology and clinical indications. Compend. Cont. Educ. 10:849-854.

Owens, C. E., R. Davis, and B. H. Smith. 1981. The psychology of euthanizing animals: The emotional components. Int. J. Stud. Anim. Prob. 2(1):19-26.

Palminteri, A. 1963. Oxymorphone, an effective analgesia in dogs and cats. J. Am. Vet. Med. Assoc. 143:160-163.

Pare, W. P., and G. B. Glavin. 1986. Restraint stress in biomedical research: A review. Neurosci. Biobehav. Rev. 10:339-370.

Paton, W. D. M. 1984. Man and Mouse: Animals in Medical Research. Oxford, N.Y..: Oxford University Press. 174 pp.

Phifer, C. B, and L. M. Terry. 1986. Use of hypothermia for general anesthesia in preweanling rodents. Physiol. Behav. 38(6):887-890.

Phillips, M. T., and J. A. Sechzer. 1989. Animal Research and Ethical Conflict: An Analysis of the Scientific Literature from 1966-1986. New York: Springer-Verlag.

PHS (Public Health Service). 1986. Public Health Service Policy on Humane Care and Use of Laboratory Animals. Implements Health Research Extension Act of 1985 (PL 99-158, Animals in Research). Washington, D.C.: U.S. Department of Health and Human Services. 28. Available from: Office for Protection from Research Risks, Building 31, Room 4B09, NIH, Bethesda, MD 20892.

Pickar, D., M. Cohen, and A. Dubois. 1983. The relationship of plasma cortisol and beta endorphin immunoreactivity to surgical stress and post-operative analgesic requirement. Gen. Hosp. Psy. 5:93-98.

Piperno, E., D. J. Ellis, S. M. Getty, and T. M. Brody. 1968. Plasma and urine levels of phenylbutazone in the horse. J. Am. Vet. Med. Assoc. 153(2):195-198.

Porro, C. A., and G. Carli. 1988. Immobilization and restraint effects on pain reactions in animals. Pain 32:289-307.

Price, E. O. 1984. Behavioral aspects of animal domestication. Q. Rev. Biol. 59:1-32.

Price, E. O. 1985. Evolutionary and ontogenetic determinants of animal suffering and well-being. Pp. 15-26 in Animal Stress, G. P. Moberg, ed. Bethesda, Md.: American Physiological Society.

Price, D. D., and R. Dubner. 1977. Neurons that subserve the sensory-discriminative aspects of pain. Pain 3:307-338.

Price, D. D., J. W. Wu, R. Dubner, and R. H. Gracely. 1977. Peripheral suppression of first pain and central summation of second pain evoked by noxious heat pulses. Pain 3:57-68.

Pry-Roberts, C., and C. C. Hug. 1984. Pp. 1-24 in Pharmacokinetics of Anesthesia. Boston, Mass.: Blackwell Scientific.

Reite, M., and T. Field, eds. 1985. The Psychobiology of Attachment and Separation. Orlando, Fla.: Academic Press. 508 pp.

Reutlinger, R. A., A. A. Karl, S. I. Vinal, and M. J. Nieser. 1980. Effects of ketamine HCl-xylazine HCl combination on cardiovascular and pulmonary values of the rhesus macaque (*Macaca mulatta*). Am. J. Vet. Res. 41:1453-1457.

Reynolds, A. K., and L. O. Randall. 1957. Morphine and Allied Drugs. Canada: University of Toronto Press.

Rigg, J. R. A., T. Y. Wong, P. Horsewood, and J. R. Hewson. 1981. Steady-state plasma fentanyl in the rabbit. Br. J. Anaesth. 53:1337-1345.

Rowsell, H. C. 1981. The present status of euthanasia by nonanesthetic gases (Letter). Can. J. Vet. 22:8.

Rubright, W. C., and C. B. Thayer. 1970. The use of Innovar-Vet® as a surgical anesthetic for the guinea pig. Lab. Anim. Sci. 20(5):989-991.

Rubright, W. C., and C. B. Thayer. 1971. Innovar-Vet®: A surgical anesthetic for the guinea pig. Practicing Vet. 43(3):16-27.

Ruda, M. A., G. J. Bennett, and R. Dubner. 1986. Neurochemistry and neural circuitry in the dorsal horn. Pp. 219-268 in Progress in Brain Research, vol. 66, P. C. Emson, M. Rossor, and M. Tohyama, eds. New York: Elsevier.

Sadove, M. S., M. Shulman, H. Shigeru, and M. Feuold. 1971. Analgesic effects of ketamine administered in subdissociative doses. Anesth. Analg. 50:452-457.

Sanford, J., and S. R. Meacham. 1978. The use of ketamine for clinical restraint of the patus monkey. Proc. AVCPT. Fall.

Sanford, T. D., and E. D. Colby. 1980. Effect of xylazine and ketamine on blood pressure, heart rate and respiratory rate in rabbits. Lab. Anim. Sci. 30(3):519-523.

Sawyer, D. C. 1988. Euthanasia agents and methods. Pp. 219-223 in Euthanasia of the Companion Animal, W. J. Kay, S. P. Cohen, C. E. Fudin, A. H. Kutscher, H. A. Nieburg, R. E. Grey, and M. M. Osman, eds. Philadelphia: The Charles Press.

Sawyer, D. C., and R. H. Rech. 1987. Analgesia and behavioral effects of butorphanol, nalbuphine, and pentazocine in the cat. J. Am. Anim. Hosp. Assoc. 23:438-446.

Sawyer, D. C., D. L. Anderson, and J. B. Scott. 1982. Cardiovascular effects and clinical use of nalbuphine in the dog. Pp. 215-216 in Proc. 1st Intl. Cong. Vet. Anesth. (abstract). J. Assoc. Vet. Anaesth. Gt. Br. Ireland. Cambridge, Eng.

Schoener, T. W. 1971. Theory of feeding strategies. Ann. Rev. Ecol. Syst. 2:369-404.

Sedgewick, C. J. 1980. Anesthesia for rabbits and rodents. Pp. 706-710 in Current Veterinary Therapy VII, R. W. Kir, ed. Philadelphia, Pa.: W. B. Saunders.

Selye, H. 1974. Stress Without Distress. Philadelphia, Pa.: J. B. Lippincott.

Short, C. E. (ed.). 1987. Principles and Practice of Veterinary Anesthesia. Baltimore, Md.: Williams & Wilkins. 669 pp.

Short, C. E., and A. Van Poznak. 1992. Animal Pain. New York: Churchill Livingstone. 587 pp.

Shucard, D. W., M. Andrew, and C. Beauford. 1975. A safe and fast-acting surgical anesthetic for use in the guinea pig. J. Appl. Physiol. 38(3):538-539.

Smith, J., and D. B. Morton. 1988. Legal protection for cephalopods? Institute of Medical Ethics' Working Party on the Ethics of Using Animals in Medical Research. London, UK.

Soma, L. R. (ed.). 1971. Textbook of Veterinary Anesthesia. Baltimore, Md.: Williams & Wilkins. 621 pp.

Soma, L. R. 1987. Assessment of animal pain in experimental animals. Lab. Anim. Sci. 37:71-74.

Soma, L. R., and A. Klide. 1987. Steady-state levels of anesthesia. J. Am. Vet. Med. Assoc. 191(10):1260-1265.

Soma, L. R., and D. R. Shields. 1964. Neuroleptanalgesia produced by fentanyl and droperidol. J. Am. Vet. Med. Assoc. 145:897.

Soma, L. R., W. J. Tierney, and N. Satoh. 1988a. Sevoflurane anesthesia in the monkey: The effects of multiples of MAC. Hiroshima J. Anesth. 24:3-14.

Soma L. R., E. Behrend, J. Rudy, and R. W. Sweeney. 1988b. Disposition and excretion of flunixin meglumine in horses. Am. J. Vet. Res. 49(11):1894-1898.

Spinelli, J. S., and H. Markowitz. 1987. Clinical recognition and anticipation of situations likely to induce suffering in animals. J. Am. Vet. Med. Assoc. 191(10):1216-1218.

Stanley W. C., and O. Elliot. 1962. Differential human handling as reinforcing events and as treatments influencing later social behavior in Basenji puppies. Psychol. Rep. 10:775-788.

Steffey, E. P. 1983. Concepts of general anesthesia and assessment of adequacy of anesthesia for animal surgery. Pp. 133-150 in Animal Pain: Perception and Alleviation, R. L. Kitchell and H. H. Erickson, eds. Bethesda, Md.: American Physiological Society.

Steffey, E. P., D. Howland, Jr., S. Giri, and E. I. Eger III. 1977. Enflurane, halothane, and isoflurane potency in horses. Am. J. Vet. Res. 38(7):1037-1039.

Stimpfel, T. M., and E. L. Gershey. 1991. Selecting anesthetic agents for human safety and animal recovery surgery. J. Fed. Am. Soc. Exptl. Biol. 5(7):2099-2104.

Stoelting, R. K. 1987. Pharmacology and Physiology in Anesthetic Practice. Philadelphia: J. B. Lippincott. 859 pp.

Stoelting, R. K., D. E. Longnecker, and E. I. Eger. 1970. Minimum alveolar concentrations in man on awakening from methoxyflurane, halothane, ether and fluroxane: MAC awake. Anesthesiology 33:5-9.

Strack, L. E., and H. M. Kaplan. 1968. Fentanyl and droperidol for surgical anesthesia of rabbits. J. Am. Vet. Med. Assoc. 153:822-825.

Szyfelbein, S., P. Osgood, and D. Carr. 1985. The assessment of pain and plasma beta endorphin immunoreactivity in burned children. Pain 22:173-182.

Tannenbaum, J. 1989. Veterinary Ethics. Baltimore, Md.: Williams & Wilkins. 358 pp.

Thurmon, J. C., A. Kumar, and R. P. Link. 1973. Evaluation of ketamine hydrochloride as an anesthetic in sheep. J. Am. Vet. Med. Assoc. 162(4):293-298.

Tomasovic, S. P., L. G. Coghlan, K. N. Gray, A. J. Mastromarino, and E. L. Travis. 1988. IACUC evaluation of experiments requiring death as an end point: A cancer center's recommendations. Lab Anim. 17(1):31-34.

Trim, C. M. 1983. Cardiopulmonary effects of butorphanol tartrate in dogs. Am. J. Vet. Res. 44(2):329-331.

Trim, C. M. 1987. Special anesthesia considerations in the ruminant. Pp. 285-300 in Principles and Practice of Veterinary Anesthesia, C. E. Short, ed. Baltimore, Md.: Williams & Wilkins.

Trim, C. M., and B. A. Gilroy. 1985. Cardiopulmonary effects of a xylazine and ketamine combination in pigs. Res. Vet. Sci. 38(1):30-34.

UFAW/WSPA (Universities Federation for Animal Welfare/World Society for the Protection of Animals). 1989. Euthanasia of Amphibians and Reptiles. Report of a Joint UFAW/WSPA Working Party. Great Britain: Universities Federation for Animal Welfare. Potters Bar, Hertz, UK. and World Society for the Protection of Animals. London, UK. 35 pp.

Valverde, A., D. H. Dyson, W. N. McDonell, and P. J. Pascoe. 1989. Use of epidural morphine in the dog for pain relief. Vet. Comp. Orthoped. Traumatol. 2:55-58.

Van Citters, L. R., D. L. Franklin, and R. F. Rushmer. 1964. Left Ventricular dynamics in dogs during anesthesia with α-chloralose and sodium pentobarbital. Am. J. Cardiol. 13:349-354.

Van Sluyters, R. C., and M. D. Oberdorfer eds. 1991. Preparation and Maintenance of Higher Mammals During Neuroscience Experiments. Report of National Institutes of Health Workshop. NIH No. 91-3207.

Vanderlip, J. E., and B. A. Gilroy. 1981. Guidelines concerning the choice and use of anesthetics, analgesics and tranquilizers in laboratory animals. Office of Campus Veterinary Science. University of California, San Diego. 1981:1-27.

Vanderwolf, C. H., G. Buzsaki, D. P. Cain, R. K. Cooley, and B. Robertson. 1988. Neocortical and hippocampal electrical activity following decapitation in the rat. Brain Res. 451:340-344.

Vernberg J. F., and W. B. Vernberg. 1970. The Animal and the Environment. New York: Holt, Rinehart & Winston.

Vierck, C. J., Jr. 1976. Extrapolations from the pain research literature to problems of adequate veterinary care. J. Am. Vet. Med. Assoc. 168(6):510-513.

Vierck, C. J., Jr., B. Y. Cooper, and R. H. Cohen. 1983. Human and nonhuman primate reactions to painful electrocutaneous stimuli and to morphine. Pp. 117-132 in Animal Pain: Perception and Alleviation, R. L. Kitchell and H. H. Ericson, eds. Bethesda, Md.: American Physiological Society.

Visalberghi, E., and A. F. Vitale. 1990. Coated nuts as an enrichment device to elicit tool use in tufted capuchins (*Cebus apella*). Zoo Biol. 9(1):65-71.

Walden, N. B. 1978. Effective sedation of rabbits, guinea pigs, rats and mice with a mixture of fentanyl and droperidol. Austral. Vet. J. 54:538-540.

Ward, G. S., D. O. Johnsen, and C. R. Roberts. 1974. The use of CI 744 as an anesthetic for laboratory animals. Lab. Anim. Sci. 24(5):737-742.

Warren, R. G. 1983. Mosby's Fundamentals of Animal Health Technology: Small Animal Anesthesia. St. Louis, Mo.: C. V. Mosby. 367 pp.

Waser, P. M., and R. H. Wiley. 1979. Mechanisms and evolution of spacing in animals. Pp. 159-223 in Handbook of Behavioral Neurobiology: Vol. 3. Social Behavior and Communication, P. Marler and J. G. Vandenbergh, eds. New York: Plenum Press.

Wass, J. A., J. R. Keene, and H. M. Kaplan. 1974. Ketamine-methoxyflurane anesthesia for rabbits. Am. J. Vet. Res. 35(2):317-318.

Weinberg, J., and S. Levine. 1980. Psychobiology of coping in animals: The effects of predictability. Pp. 39-59 in Coping and Health, S. Levine and H. Ursin, eds. New York: Plenum Press.

Weiskopf R. B., and M. S. Bogetz. 1984. Minimum alveolar concentrations (MAC) of halothane and nitrous oxide in swine. Anesth. Analg. 63(5):529-532.

Wemelsfelder, F. 1990. Boredom and laboratory animal welfare. Pp. 243-272 in The Experimental Animal in Biomedical Research, B. E. Rollin, ed. Boca Raton, Fla.: CRC Press.

White, P. F., R. R. Johnston, and E. I. Eger. 1974. Determination of anesthetic requirement in rats. Anesthesiology 40(1):52-57.

White, P. F., R. R. Johnston, and C. R. Pudwill. 1975. Interaction of ketamine and halothane in rats. Anesthesiology 42(2):179-186.

White, S. D. 1990. Naltrexone for the treatment of acral lick dermatitis in dogs. J. Am. Vet. Med. Assoc. 196(7):1073-1076.

Wigglesworth, V. B. 1980. Do insects feel pain? Antenna 4:8-9.

Willis, W. D. 1985. The Pain System—The Neural Basis of Nociceptive Transmission in the Mammalian Nervous System. New York: S. Karger. 346 pp.

Wilson, P., and A. M. Wheatley. 1981. Ketamine hydrochloride in the laboratory rat. Lab. Anim. 15(4):349.

Winters, W. D., T. Ferrar-Allado, C. Guzman-Flores, and M. Alcarez. 1972. The cataleptic state induced by ketamine: A review of the neuropharmacology of anesthesia. Neuropharmacology 1:303-315.

Wixson, S. K., W. J. White, H. C. Hughes, Jr., C. M. Lang, and W. K. Marshall. 1987a. A comparison of pentobarbital, fentanyl-droperidol, ketamine-xylazine and ketamine-diazepam anesthesia in adult male rats. Lab. Anim. Sci. 37(6):726-730.

Wixson, S. K., W. J. White, H. C. Hughes, Jr., W. K. Marshall, and C. M. Lang. 1987b. The effects of pentobarbital, fentanyl-droperidol, ketamine-xylazine and ketamine-diazepam on noxious stimulus perception in adult male rats. Lab. Anim. Sci. 37(6):731-735.

Wixson, S. K., W. J. White, H. C. Hughes, Jr., C. M. Lang, and W. K. Marshall. 1987c. The effects of pentobarbital, fentanyl-droperidol, ketamine-xylazine and ketamine-diazepam on arterial blood pH, blood gases, mean arterial blood pressure and heart rate in adult male rats. Lab. Anim. Sci. 37(6):736-742.

Wolff, B. B. 1978. Behavioural measurement of human pain. Pp. 129-168 in The Psychology of Pain, R. A. Sternbach, ed. New York: Raven Press.

Wolfle, T. L. 1985. Laboratory animal technicians: Their role in stress reduction and human-companion animal bonding. Vet. Clin. N. Am.: Small Anim. Pract. 15(2):449-454.

Wolfle, T. L. 1987. Control of stress using non-drug approaches. J. Am. Vet. Med. Assoc. 191(10):1219-1221.

Wolfle, T. L., and J.C. Liebeskind. 1983. Stimulation-produced analgesia. Pp. 107-115 in Animal Pain: Perception and Alleviation. Bethesda, Md.: American Physiological Society.

Woolfson, M. W., J. A. Foran, H. M. Freedman, P. A. Moore, L. B. Shulman, and P. A. Schnitman. 1980. Immobilization of baboons (*Papio anubis*) using ketamine and diazepam. Lab. Anim. Sci. 30(5):902-904.

Wright, M. 1982. Pharmacologic effects of ketamine and its use in veterinary medicine. J. Am. Vet. Med. Assoc. 180:1462-1470.

Wright, E. M., K. L. Marcella, and J. F. Woodson. 1985. Animal pain: Evaluation and control. Lab Anim. 14(4):20-36.

Yaksh, T. L., and T. A. Rudy. 1978. Narcotic analgesia: CNS sites and mechanisms of action as revealed by intracerebral injection techniques. Pain 4:299-359.

Yates, W. D. 1973. Clinical uses of xylazine: A new drug for old problems. Vet./Small Anim. Clin. 63:483-486.

Zimmermann, M. 1984. Neurobiological concepts of pain, its assessment and therapy. Pp. 15-35 in Pain Measurement in Man: Neurophysiological Correlates of Pain, B. Bromm, ed. Amsterdam: Elsevier Press.

Index

A

Abdominal surgery, 41
Acetaminophen, 76
Acetylpromazine, 87, 88
Acupuncture, 84
Adaptation, 2, 7-9, 18, 29-31, 100-101
α_2-Adrenergic agonists, 90-92
Adrenocorticotropic hormone (ACTH), 51
Age, *see* Maturity
Aggression, 20-21, 95
Alopecia, 103
American Association for the
    Accreditation of Laboratory Animal
    Care (AAALAC), 1
Amphibians, euthanasia of, 107, 113, 115-
    116
Amphibians: Guidelines for the Breeding,
    Care, and Management of Laboratory
    Animals, 116
Analgesics, 36, 57, 58, 105
    see also Nonsteroidal anti-inflammatory
      drugs; Opioids
Anderson, M.D., Cancer Center,
    University of Texas, 103

Anemia, 103
Anesthesia, 54, 56-69, 78-79
    and euthanasia, 106-107, 113, 116
    and muscle relaxants, 79-82
    and salivation, 81
Anesthesia in Fish, 116
Animal Welfare Regulations, 1, 96
Antibody production, 101
Antipsychotics, 86-89
Anxiety, 6-7, 105, 108, 111
Anxiolytics, *see* Sedatives and
    tranquilizers
Ascites, 103
Atropine, 64
Atypical behavior, 22, 48-50
Autolysis, 102-103
Avoidance behavior, 2, 6, 54
Azaperone, 89

B

Barbiturates, 61-63, 90
    for euthanasia, 111-112, 113, 116
Behavior, adaptive, 2, 7-9, 18, 29, 30-31,
    100-101

NATIONAL ACADEMY PRESS
The National Academy Press was created by the
National Academy of Sciences to publish the reports
issued by the Academy and by the National Academy
of Engineering, the Institute of Medicine, and the
National Research Council, all operating under the
charter granted to the National Academy of Sciences
by the Congress of the United States.